JOLPIC'S

Multiplication

Timed Tests

WORKBOOK

FOR GRADES 1-2

JOLPIC KIDZ

JOLPIC KIDZ

Jolpic Kidz is a publishing company of educational books for kids. To receive free catalogue,
Send mail us at: *jolpic@gmail.com*

JOLPIC's Multiplication Timed Tests Workbook for Grades 1-2

This book belongs to

- - - - - - - - - - - - - - - - - -

- - - - - - - - - - - - - - - - - -

CONTENTS

1.	2.	3.	4.	5.
3 × 1	4 × 2	3 × 4	1 × 2	0 × 0

6.	7.	8.	9.	10.
4 × 1	3 × 2	5 × 1	3 × 7	9 × 2

11.	12.	13.	14.	15.
4 × 3	5 × 0	1 × 6	6 × 4	4 × 8

16.	17.	18.	19.	20.
6 × 2	7 × 3	7 × 1	8 × 2	2 × 2

21.	22.	23.	24.	25.
9 × 4	8 × 7	9 × 0	9 × 1	5 × 2

Marks obtained: ___ Comment: ___

TIMED TEST

1. 2 × 5	2. 3 × 4	3. 7 × 3	4. 5 × 3	5. 3 × 6
6. 5 × 1	7. 0 × 5	8. 6 × 5	9. 0 × 1	10. 3 × 3
11. 7 × 6	12. 3 × 1	13. 4 × 2	14. 1 × 1	15. 7 × 7
16. 3 × 7	17. 4 × 1	18. 1 × 8	19. 9 × 8	20. 5 × 9
21. 6 × 7	22. 9 × 9	23. 7 × 9	24. 6 × 6	25. 7 × 5

TIMED TEST

1. $\begin{array}{r} 3 \\ \times\ 5 \\ \hline \end{array}$	2. $\begin{array}{r} 3 \\ \times\ 4 \\ \hline \end{array}$	3. $\begin{array}{r} 9 \\ \times\ 5 \\ \hline \end{array}$	4. $\begin{array}{r} 5 \\ \times\ 7 \\ \hline \end{array}$	5. $\begin{array}{r} 5 \\ \times\ 8 \\ \hline \end{array}$
6. $\begin{array}{r} 2 \\ \times\ 7 \\ \hline \end{array}$	7. $\begin{array}{r} 7 \\ \times\ 7 \\ \hline \end{array}$	8. $\begin{array}{r} 9 \\ \times\ 8 \\ \hline \end{array}$	9. $\begin{array}{r} 3 \\ \times\ 8 \\ \hline \end{array}$	10. $\begin{array}{r} 4 \\ \times\ 6 \\ \hline \end{array}$
11. $\begin{array}{r} 3 \\ \times\ 3 \\ \hline \end{array}$	12. $\begin{array}{r} 6 \\ \times\ 5 \\ \hline \end{array}$	13. $\begin{array}{r} 2 \\ \times\ 5 \\ \hline \end{array}$	14. $\begin{array}{r} 7 \\ \times\ 8 \\ \hline \end{array}$	15. $\begin{array}{r} 7 \\ \times\ 9 \\ \hline \end{array}$
16. $\begin{array}{r} 6 \\ \times\ 8 \\ \hline \end{array}$	17. $\begin{array}{r} 8 \\ \times\ 4 \\ \hline \end{array}$	18. $\begin{array}{r} 5 \\ \times\ 5 \\ \hline \end{array}$	19. $\begin{array}{r} 5 \\ \times\ 9 \\ \hline \end{array}$	20. $\begin{array}{r} 3 \\ \times\ 9 \\ \hline \end{array}$
21. $\begin{array}{r} 8 \\ \times\ 2 \\ \hline \end{array}$	22. $\begin{array}{r} 8 \\ \times\ 8 \\ \hline \end{array}$	23. $\begin{array}{r} 9 \\ \times\ 4 \\ \hline \end{array}$	24. $\begin{array}{r} 4 \\ \times\ 5 \\ \hline \end{array}$	25. $\begin{array}{r} 3 \\ \times\ 6 \\ \hline \end{array}$

Marks obtained:

Comment:

Name: ____________________ Date: __ / __ / __

Marks: ____________

TIMED TEST

Time: ____________

1. $\begin{array}{r} 6 \\ \times\ 9 \\ \hline \end{array}$	2. $\begin{array}{r} 4 \\ \times\ 3 \\ \hline \end{array}$	3. $\begin{array}{r} 3 \\ \times\ 2 \\ \hline \end{array}$	4. $\begin{array}{r} 8 \\ \times\ 3 \\ \hline \end{array}$	5. $\begin{array}{r} 7 \\ \times\ 5 \\ \hline \end{array}$
6. $\begin{array}{r} 2 \\ \times\ 3 \\ \hline \end{array}$	7. $\begin{array}{r} 6 \\ \times\ 2 \\ \hline \end{array}$	8. $\begin{array}{r} 8 \\ \times\ 9 \\ \hline \end{array}$	9. $\begin{array}{r} 5 \\ \times\ 6 \\ \hline \end{array}$	10. $\begin{array}{r} 4 \\ \times\ 4 \\ \hline \end{array}$
11. $\begin{array}{r} 4 \\ \times\ 8 \\ \hline \end{array}$	12. $\begin{array}{r} 4 \\ \times\ 6 \\ \hline \end{array}$	13. $\begin{array}{r} 4 \\ \times\ 7 \\ \hline \end{array}$	14. $\begin{array}{r} 6 \\ \times\ 6 \\ \hline \end{array}$	15. $\begin{array}{r} 9 \\ \times\ 7 \\ \hline \end{array}$
16. $\begin{array}{r} 3 \\ \times\ 7 \\ \hline \end{array}$	17. $\begin{array}{r} 6 \\ \times\ 7 \\ \hline \end{array}$	18. $\begin{array}{r} 7 \\ \times\ 2 \\ \hline \end{array}$	19. $\begin{array}{r} 7 \\ \times\ 7 \\ \hline \end{array}$	20. $\begin{array}{r} 9 \\ \times\ 5 \\ \hline \end{array}$
21. $\begin{array}{r} 3 \\ \times\ 5 \\ \hline \end{array}$	22. $\begin{array}{r} 5 \\ \times\ 5 \\ \hline \end{array}$	23. $\begin{array}{r} 2 \\ \times\ 9 \\ \hline \end{array}$	24. $\begin{array}{r} 4 \\ \times\ 5 \\ \hline \end{array}$	25. $\begin{array}{r} 0 \\ \times\ 6 \\ \hline \end{array}$

Marks obtained: ____________ Comment: ____________

7

TIMED TEST

Name: Date: /   /

Marks: Time:

1. $\begin{array}{r} 1 \\ \times\ 7 \\ \hline \end{array}$	2. $\begin{array}{r} 2 \\ \times\ 6 \\ \hline \end{array}$	3. $\begin{array}{r} 1 \\ \times\ 8 \\ \hline \end{array}$	4. $\begin{array}{r} 5 \\ \times\ 7 \\ \hline \end{array}$	5. $\begin{array}{r} 9 \\ \times\ 7 \\ \hline \end{array}$
6. $\begin{array}{r} 9 \\ \times\ 6 \\ \hline \end{array}$	7. $\begin{array}{r} 2 \\ \times\ 3 \\ \hline \end{array}$	8. $\begin{array}{r} 1 \\ \times\ 1 \\ \hline \end{array}$	9. $\begin{array}{r} 8 \\ \times\ 2 \\ \hline \end{array}$	10. $\begin{array}{r} 3 \\ \times\ 6 \\ \hline \end{array}$
11. $\begin{array}{r} 0 \\ \times\ 4 \\ \hline \end{array}$	12. $\begin{array}{r} 5 \\ \times\ 6 \\ \hline \end{array}$	13. $\begin{array}{r} 9 \\ \times\ 9 \\ \hline \end{array}$	14. $\begin{array}{r} 2 \\ \times\ 9 \\ \hline \end{array}$	15. $\begin{array}{r} 8 \\ \times\ 3 \\ \hline \end{array}$
16. $\begin{array}{r} 4 \\ \times\ 5 \\ \hline \end{array}$	17. $\begin{array}{r} 5 \\ \times\ 8 \\ \hline \end{array}$	18. $\begin{array}{r} 4 \\ \times\ 9 \\ \hline \end{array}$	19. $\begin{array}{r} 2 \\ \times\ 7 \\ \hline \end{array}$	20. $\begin{array}{r} 3 \\ \times\ 5 \\ \hline \end{array}$
21. $\begin{array}{r} 6 \\ \times\ 8 \\ \hline \end{array}$	22. $\begin{array}{r} 7 \\ \times\ 7 \\ \hline \end{array}$	23. $\begin{array}{r} 7 \\ \times\ 8 \\ \hline \end{array}$	24. $\begin{array}{r} 5 \\ \times\ 9 \\ \hline \end{array}$	25. $\begin{array}{r} 4 \\ \times\ 8 \\ \hline \end{array}$

8

Marks obtained: Comment:

TIMED TEST

1. 2 × 5	2. 1 × 2	3. 2 × 7

1. 2 × 5 = ___
2. 1 × 2 = ___
3. 2 × 7 = ___
4. 4 × 5 = ___
5. 9 × 5 = ___
6. 9 × 7 = ___
7. 7 × 5 = ___
8. 3 × 9 = ___
9. 7 × 8 = ___
10. 9 × 2 = ___
11. 2 × 4 = ___
12. 5 × 6 = ___
13. 7 × 4 = ___
14. 7 × 3 = ___
15. 6 × 3 = ___
16. 8 × 1 = ___
17. 8 × 5 = ___
18. 6 × 5 = ___
19. 4 × 8 = ___
20. 4 × 6 = ___
21. 0 × 7 = ___
22. 9 × 9 = ___
23. 2 × 6 = ___
24. 3 × 5 = ___
25. 6 × 9 = ___

1.
$$\begin{array}{r} 3 \\ \times\ 5 \\ \hline \end{array}$$

2.
$$\begin{array}{r} 9 \\ \times\ 6 \\ \hline \end{array}$$

3.
$$\begin{array}{r} 5 \\ \times\ 9 \\ \hline \end{array}$$

4.
$$\begin{array}{r} 8 \\ \times\ 7 \\ \hline \end{array}$$

5.
$$\begin{array}{r} 5 \\ \times\ 6 \\ \hline \end{array}$$

6.
$$\begin{array}{r} 8 \\ \times\ 9 \\ \hline \end{array}$$

7.
$$\begin{array}{r} 3 \\ \times\ 8 \\ \hline \end{array}$$

8.
$$\begin{array}{r} 7 \\ \times\ 9 \\ \hline \end{array}$$

9.
$$\begin{array}{r} 3 \\ \times\ 4 \\ \hline \end{array}$$

10.
$$\begin{array}{r} 4 \\ \times\ 4 \\ \hline \end{array}$$

11.
$$\begin{array}{r} 6 \\ \times\ 2 \\ \hline \end{array}$$

12.
$$\begin{array}{r} 1 \\ \times\ 6 \\ \hline \end{array}$$

13.
$$\begin{array}{r} 2 \\ \times\ 5 \\ \hline \end{array}$$

14.
$$\begin{array}{r} 5 \\ \times\ 8 \\ \hline \end{array}$$

15.
$$\begin{array}{r} 7 \\ \times\ 5 \\ \hline \end{array}$$

16.
$$\begin{array}{r} 1 \\ \times\ 9 \\ \hline \end{array}$$

17.
$$\begin{array}{r} 4 \\ \times\ 5 \\ \hline \end{array}$$

18.
$$\begin{array}{r} 9 \\ \times\ 4 \\ \hline \end{array}$$

19.
$$\begin{array}{r} 3 \\ \times\ 2 \\ \hline \end{array}$$

20.
$$\begin{array}{r} 7 \\ \times\ 7 \\ \hline \end{array}$$

21.
$$\begin{array}{r} 4 \\ \times\ 7 \\ \hline \end{array}$$

22.
$$\begin{array}{r} 6 \\ \times\ 4 \\ \hline \end{array}$$

23.
$$\begin{array}{r} 8 \\ \times\ 8 \\ \hline \end{array}$$

24.
$$\begin{array}{r} 6 \\ \times\ 8 \\ \hline \end{array}$$

25.
$$\begin{array}{r} 0 \\ \times\ 1 \\ \hline \end{array}$$

Marks obtained: Comment:

1. 9 × 9	2. 9 × 2	3. 8 × 6	4. 2 × 3	5. 3 × 6
6. 6 × 6	7. 4 × 9	8. 8 × 4	9. 6 × 9	10. 5 × 9
11. 7 × 4	12. 3 × 9	13. 4 × 6	14. 0 × 4	15. 9 × 5
16. 3 × 7	17. 9 × 9	18. 8 × 8	19. 8 × 5	20. 2 × 4
21. 5 × 5	22. 5 × 3	23. 4 × 5	24. 5 × 6	25. 7 × 9

Marks obtained: Comment:

Marks: # TIMED TEST   Time:

1. $\begin{array}{r} 9 \\ \times\ 4 \\ \hline \end{array}$	2. $\begin{array}{r} 5 \\ \times\ 1 \\ \hline \end{array}$	3. $\begin{array}{r} 4 \\ \times\ 6 \\ \hline \end{array}$	4. $\begin{array}{r} 3 \\ \times\ 6 \\ \hline \end{array}$	5. $\begin{array}{r} 2 \\ \times\ 8 \\ \hline \end{array}$
6. $\begin{array}{r} 2 \\ \times\ 6 \\ \hline \end{array}$	7. $\begin{array}{r} 5 \\ \times\ 5 \\ \hline \end{array}$	8. $\begin{array}{r} 1 \\ \times\ 7 \\ \hline \end{array}$	9. $\begin{array}{r} 8 \\ \times\ 5 \\ \hline \end{array}$	10. $\begin{array}{r} 9 \\ \times\ 5 \\ \hline \end{array}$
11. $\begin{array}{r} 4 \\ \times\ 5 \\ \hline \end{array}$	12. $\begin{array}{r} 8 \\ \times\ 3 \\ \hline \end{array}$	13. $\begin{array}{r} 3 \\ \times\ 5 \\ \hline \end{array}$	14. $\begin{array}{r} 9 \\ \times\ 8 \\ \hline \end{array}$	15. $\begin{array}{r} 3 \\ \times\ 9 \\ \hline \end{array}$
16. $\begin{array}{r} 4 \\ \times\ 8 \\ \hline \end{array}$	17. $\begin{array}{r} 8 \\ \times\ 6 \\ \hline \end{array}$	18. $\begin{array}{r} 8 \\ \times\ 8 \\ \hline \end{array}$	19. $\begin{array}{r} 7 \\ \times\ 6 \\ \hline \end{array}$	20. $\begin{array}{r} 6 \\ \times\ 9 \\ \hline \end{array}$
21. $\begin{array}{r} 7 \\ \times\ 8 \\ \hline \end{array}$	22. $\begin{array}{r} 2 \\ \times\ 7 \\ \hline \end{array}$	23. $\begin{array}{r} 6 \\ \times\ 5 \\ \hline \end{array}$	24. $\begin{array}{r} 3 \\ \times\ 7 \\ \hline \end{array}$	25. $\begin{array}{r} 0 \\ \times\ 6 \\ \hline \end{array}$

12

Marks obtained: Comment:

TIMED TEST

Marks: Time:

1. $\begin{array}{r} 2 \\ \times\ 3 \\ \hline \end{array}$

2. $\begin{array}{r} 6 \\ \times\ 8 \\ \hline \end{array}$

3. $\begin{array}{r} 5 \\ \times\ 1 \\ \hline \end{array}$

4. $\begin{array}{r} 9 \\ \times\ 8 \\ \hline \end{array}$

5. $\begin{array}{r} 3 \\ \times\ 9 \\ \hline \end{array}$

6. $\begin{array}{r} 2 \\ \times\ 7 \\ \hline \end{array}$

7. $\begin{array}{r} 2 \\ \times\ 9 \\ \hline \end{array}$

8. $\begin{array}{r} 3 \\ \times\ 8 \\ \hline \end{array}$

9. $\begin{array}{r} 6 \\ \times\ 3 \\ \hline \end{array}$

10. $\begin{array}{r} 5 \\ \times\ 6 \\ \hline \end{array}$

11. $\begin{array}{r} 9 \\ \times\ 7 \\ \hline \end{array}$

12. $\begin{array}{r} 4 \\ \times\ 6 \\ \hline \end{array}$

13. $\begin{array}{r} 6 \\ \times\ 9 \\ \hline \end{array}$

14. $\begin{array}{r} 4 \\ \times\ 2 \\ \hline \end{array}$

15. $\begin{array}{r} 7 \\ \times\ 8 \\ \hline \end{array}$

16. $\begin{array}{r} 3 \\ \times\ 4 \\ \hline \end{array}$

17. $\begin{array}{r} 5 \\ \times\ 7 \\ \hline \end{array}$

18. $\begin{array}{r} 4 \\ \times\ 8 \\ \hline \end{array}$

19. $\begin{array}{r} 6 \\ \times\ 6 \\ \hline \end{array}$

20. $\begin{array}{r} 7 \\ \times\ 7 \\ \hline \end{array}$

21. $\begin{array}{r} 9 \\ \times\ 9 \\ \hline \end{array}$

22. $\begin{array}{r} 6 \\ \times\ 7 \\ \hline \end{array}$

23. $\begin{array}{r} 4 \\ \times\ 5 \\ \hline \end{array}$

24. $\begin{array}{r} 5 \\ \times\ 8 \\ \hline \end{array}$

25. $\begin{array}{r} 5 \\ \times\ 9 \\ \hline \end{array}$

TIMED TEST

1.
$$\begin{array}{r} 4 \\ \times\ 8 \\ \hline \end{array}$$

2.
$$\begin{array}{r} 1 \\ \times\ 9 \\ \hline \end{array}$$

3.
$$\begin{array}{r} 6 \\ \times\ 3 \\ \hline \end{array}$$

4.
$$\begin{array}{r} 2 \\ \times\ 4 \\ \hline \end{array}$$

5.
$$\begin{array}{r} 4 \\ \times\ 9 \\ \hline \end{array}$$

6.
$$\begin{array}{r} 6 \\ \times\ 9 \\ \hline \end{array}$$

7.
$$\begin{array}{r} 9 \\ \times\ 7 \\ \hline \end{array}$$

8.
$$\begin{array}{r} 4 \\ \times\ 7 \\ \hline \end{array}$$

9.
$$\begin{array}{r} 3 \\ \times\ 5 \\ \hline \end{array}$$

10.
$$\begin{array}{r} 5 \\ \times\ 4 \\ \hline \end{array}$$

11.
$$\begin{array}{r} 6 \\ \times\ 8 \\ \hline \end{array}$$

12.
$$\begin{array}{r} 2 \\ \times\ 9 \\ \hline \end{array}$$

13.
$$\begin{array}{r} 3 \\ \times\ 8 \\ \hline \end{array}$$

14.
$$\begin{array}{r} 8 \\ \times\ 9 \\ \hline \end{array}$$

15.
$$\begin{array}{r} 9 \\ \times\ 9 \\ \hline \end{array}$$

16.
$$\begin{array}{r} 2 \\ \times\ 8 \\ \hline \end{array}$$

17.
$$\begin{array}{r} 5 \\ \times\ 2 \\ \hline \end{array}$$

18.
$$\begin{array}{r} 7 \\ \times\ 3 \\ \hline \end{array}$$

19.
$$\begin{array}{r} 4 \\ \times\ 4 \\ \hline \end{array}$$

20.
$$\begin{array}{r} 7 \\ \times\ 7 \\ \hline \end{array}$$

21.
$$\begin{array}{r} 5 \\ \times\ 6 \\ \hline \end{array}$$

22.
$$\begin{array}{r} 7 \\ \times\ 8 \\ \hline \end{array}$$

23.
$$\begin{array}{r} 1 \\ \times\ 1 \\ \hline \end{array}$$

24.
$$\begin{array}{r} 8 \\ \times\ 5 \\ \hline \end{array}$$

25.
$$\begin{array}{r} 6 \\ \times\ 4 \\ \hline \end{array}$$

Marks obtained: Comment:

TIMED TEST

1.
$$\begin{array}{r} 2 \\ \times\ 7 \\ \hline \end{array}$$

2.
$$\begin{array}{r} 5 \\ \times\ 4 \\ \hline \end{array}$$

3.
$$\begin{array}{r} 6 \\ \times\ 5 \\ \hline \end{array}$$

4.
$$\begin{array}{r} 3 \\ \times\ 9 \\ \hline \end{array}$$

5.
$$\begin{array}{r} 1 \\ \times\ 2 \\ \hline \end{array}$$

6.
$$\begin{array}{r} 7 \\ \times\ 5 \\ \hline \end{array}$$

7.
$$\begin{array}{r} 7 \\ \times\ 1 \\ \hline \end{array}$$

8.
$$\begin{array}{r} 9 \\ \times\ 6 \\ \hline \end{array}$$

9.
$$\begin{array}{r} 3 \\ \times\ 2 \\ \hline \end{array}$$

10.
$$\begin{array}{r} 7 \\ \times\ 9 \\ \hline \end{array}$$

11.
$$\begin{array}{r} 5 \\ \times\ 5 \\ \hline \end{array}$$

12.
$$\begin{array}{r} 5 \\ \times\ 8 \\ \hline \end{array}$$

13.
$$\begin{array}{r} 2 \\ \times\ 6 \\ \hline \end{array}$$

14.
$$\begin{array}{r} 7 \\ \times\ 8 \\ \hline \end{array}$$

15.
$$\begin{array}{r} 3 \\ \times\ 5 \\ \hline \end{array}$$

16.
$$\begin{array}{r} 2 \\ \times\ 4 \\ \hline \end{array}$$

17.
$$\begin{array}{r} 8 \\ \times\ 6 \\ \hline \end{array}$$

18.
$$\begin{array}{r} 3 \\ \times\ 7 \\ \hline \end{array}$$

19.
$$\begin{array}{r} 5 \\ \times\ 9 \\ \hline \end{array}$$

20.
$$\begin{array}{r} 3 \\ \times\ 3 \\ \hline \end{array}$$

21.
$$\begin{array}{r} 4 \\ \times\ 9 \\ \hline \end{array}$$

22.
$$\begin{array}{r} 8 \\ \times\ 9 \\ \hline \end{array}$$

23.
$$\begin{array}{r} 6 \\ \times\ 4 \\ \hline \end{array}$$

24.
$$\begin{array}{r} 8 \\ \times\ 8 \\ \hline \end{array}$$

25.
$$\begin{array}{r} 5 \\ \times\ 0 \\ \hline \end{array}$$

Marks obtained: Comment:

TIMED TEST

1. $\begin{array}{r} 5 \\ \times\ 5 \\ \hline \end{array}$	**2.** $\begin{array}{r} 7 \\ \times\ 7 \\ \hline \end{array}$	**3.** $\begin{array}{r} 6 \\ \times\ 8 \\ \hline \end{array}$	**4.** $\begin{array}{r} 6 \\ \times\ 3 \\ \hline \end{array}$	**5.** $\begin{array}{r} 3 \\ \times\ 8 \\ \hline \end{array}$
6. $\begin{array}{r} 7 \\ \times\ 9 \\ \hline \end{array}$	**7.** $\begin{array}{r} 4 \\ \times\ 3 \\ \hline \end{array}$	**8.** $\begin{array}{r} 7 \\ \times\ 8 \\ \hline \end{array}$	**9.** $\begin{array}{r} 2 \\ \times\ 9 \\ \hline \end{array}$	**10.** $\begin{array}{r} 7 \\ \times\ 2 \\ \hline \end{array}$
11. $\begin{array}{r} 3 \\ \times\ 3 \\ \hline \end{array}$	**12.** $\begin{array}{r} 5 \\ \times\ 4 \\ \hline \end{array}$	**13.** $\begin{array}{r} 7 \\ \times\ 5 \\ \hline \end{array}$	**14.** $\begin{array}{r} 9 \\ \times\ 6 \\ \hline \end{array}$	**15.** $\begin{array}{r} 2 \\ \times\ 5 \\ \hline \end{array}$
16. $\begin{array}{r} 2 \\ \times\ 7 \\ \hline \end{array}$	**17.** $\begin{array}{r} 5 \\ \times\ 9 \\ \hline \end{array}$	**18.** $\begin{array}{r} 9 \\ \times\ 9 \\ \hline \end{array}$	**19.** $\begin{array}{r} 5 \\ \times\ 6 \\ \hline \end{array}$	**20.** $\begin{array}{r} 7 \\ \times\ 3 \\ \hline \end{array}$
21. $\begin{array}{r} 5 \\ \times\ 8 \\ \hline \end{array}$	**22.** $\begin{array}{r} 6 \\ \times\ 4 \\ \hline \end{array}$	**23.** $\begin{array}{r} 8 \\ \times\ 9 \\ \hline \end{array}$	**24.** $\begin{array}{r} 9 \\ \times\ 4 \\ \hline \end{array}$	**25.** $\begin{array}{r} 7 \\ \times\ 6 \\ \hline \end{array}$

16

Marks obtained: Comment:

TIMED TEST

1. 6 × 7 = ___

2. 5 × 9 = ___

3. 7 × 4 = ___

4. 9 × 6 = ___

5. 8 × 8 = ___

6. 4 × 3 = ___

7. 2 × 4 = ___

8. 8 × 2 = ___

9. 4 × 5 = ___

10. 7 × 7 = ___

11. 6 × 3 = ___

12. 9 × 7 = ___

13. 8 × 4 = ___

14. 8 × 7 = ___

15. 3 × 2 = ___

16. 5 × 5 = ___

17. 8 × 5 = ___

18. 9 × 2 = ___

19. 5 × 6 = ___

20. 9 × 9 = ___

21. 3 × 7 = ___

22. 3 × 5 = ___

23. 5 × 7 = ___

24. 6 × 6 = ___

25. 2 × 1 = ___

TIMED TEST

1.
$$\begin{array}{r} 3 \\ \times\ 9 \\ \hline \end{array}$$

2.
$$\begin{array}{r} 6 \\ \times\ 9 \\ \hline \end{array}$$

3.
$$\begin{array}{r} 9 \\ \times\ 5 \\ \hline \end{array}$$

4.
$$\begin{array}{r} 5 \\ \times\ 3 \\ \hline \end{array}$$

5.
$$\begin{array}{r} 7 \\ \times\ 9 \\ \hline \end{array}$$

6.
$$\begin{array}{r} 7 \\ \times\ 7 \\ \hline \end{array}$$

7.
$$\begin{array}{r} 8 \\ \times\ 3 \\ \hline \end{array}$$

8.
$$\begin{array}{r} 4 \\ \times\ 9 \\ \hline \end{array}$$

9.
$$\begin{array}{r} 5 \\ \times\ 7 \\ \hline \end{array}$$

10.
$$\begin{array}{r} 9 \\ \times\ 8 \\ \hline \end{array}$$

11.
$$\begin{array}{r} 6 \\ \times\ 2 \\ \hline \end{array}$$

12.
$$\begin{array}{r} 6 \\ \times\ 4 \\ \hline \end{array}$$

13.
$$\begin{array}{r} 5 \\ \times\ 5 \\ \hline \end{array}$$

14.
$$\begin{array}{r} 8 \\ \times\ 5 \\ \hline \end{array}$$

15.
$$\begin{array}{r} 6 \\ \times\ 7 \\ \hline \end{array}$$

16.
$$\begin{array}{r} 2 \\ \times\ 3 \\ \hline \end{array}$$

17.
$$\begin{array}{r} 2 \\ \times\ 7 \\ \hline \end{array}$$

18.
$$\begin{array}{r} 3 \\ \times\ 6 \\ \hline \end{array}$$

19.
$$\begin{array}{r} 5 \\ \times\ 4 \\ \hline \end{array}$$

20.
$$\begin{array}{r} 2 \\ \times\ 4 \\ \hline \end{array}$$

21.
$$\begin{array}{r} 4 \\ \times\ 4 \\ \hline \end{array}$$

22.
$$\begin{array}{r} 3 \\ \times\ 3 \\ \hline \end{array}$$

23.
$$\begin{array}{r} 6 \\ \times\ 5 \\ \hline \end{array}$$

24.
$$\begin{array}{r} 8 \\ \times\ 7 \\ \hline \end{array}$$

25.
$$\begin{array}{r} 9 \\ \times\ 2 \\ \hline \end{array}$$

Marks obtained: Comment:

TIMED TEST

1. $\begin{array}{r} 3 \\ \times\ 6 \\ \hline \end{array}$	2. $\begin{array}{r} 5 \\ \times\ 6 \\ \hline \end{array}$	3. $\begin{array}{r} 3 \\ \times\ 7 \\ \hline \end{array}$

1. 3 × 6 =
2. 5 × 6 =
3. 3 × 7 =
4. 9 × 6 =
5. 7 × 8 =
6. 3 × 9 =
7. 7 × 6 =
8. 3 × 3 =
9. 7 × 7 =
10. 5 × 3 =
11. 5 × 5 =
12. 7 × 9 =
13. 4 × 7 =
14. 8 × 4 =
15. 8 × 9 =
16. 4 × 2 =
17. 9 × 4 =
18. 5 × 4 =
19. 8 × 6 =
20. 5 × 9 =
21. 5 × 8 =
22. 9 × 9 =
23. 5 × 1 =
24. 6 × 6 =
25. 2 × 8 =

TIMED TEST

1.	7 × 5
2.	9 × 9
3.	4 × 9
4.	8 × 4
5.	3 × 3
6.	6 × 3
7.	3 × 7
8.	2 × 9
9.	6 × 4
10.	2 × 5
11.	4 × 7
12.	6 × 7
13.	8 × 6
14.	2 × 2
15.	3 × 2
16.	5 × 9
17.	8 × 5
18.	6 × 5
19.	7 × 8
20.	2 × 4
21.	3 × 6
22.	7 × 7
23.	7 × 9
24.	3 × 8
25.	8 × 8

Marks obtained: _____ Comment: _____

20

TIMED TEST

1.
$$16 \times 8$$

2.
$$31 \times 9$$

3.
$$29 \times 3$$

4.
$$65 \times 8$$

5.
$$54 \times 6$$

6.
$$58 \times 5$$

7.
$$86 \times 2$$

8.
$$29 \times 7$$

9.
$$46 \times 6$$

10.
$$47 \times 3$$

11.
$$41 \times 7$$

12.
$$95 \times 9$$

13.
$$69 \times 6$$

14.
$$16 \times 3$$

15.
$$72 \times 5$$

16.
$$66 \times 9$$

17.
$$58 \times 6$$

18.
$$63 \times 7$$

19.
$$78 \times 8$$

20.
$$30 \times 7$$

21.
$$97 \times 4$$

22.
$$95 \times 9$$

23.
$$35 \times 2$$

24.
$$75 \times 8$$

25.
$$53 \times 4$$

Marks obtained: Comment:

Marks:

TIMED TEST

Time:

1. 28 × 7	2. 94 × 5	3. 35 × 3	4. 38 × 9	5. 23 × 9
6. 55 × 3	7. 62 × 3	8. 19 × 9	9. 42 × 4	10. 61 × 3
11. 41 × 8	12. 38 × 4	13. 90 × 5	14. 56 × 9	15. 91 × 7
16. 86 × 4	17. 35 × 6	18. 26 × 5	19. 27 × 8	20. 94 × 4
21. 17 × 4	22. 96 × 9	23. 66 × 6	24. 67 × 5	25. 44 × 7

Marks obtained: Comment:

TIMED TEST

1. $\begin{array}{r} 17 \\ \times\ \ 8 \\ \hline \end{array}$	2. $\begin{array}{r} 54 \\ \times\ \ 6 \\ \hline \end{array}$	3. $\begin{array}{r} 60 \\ \times\ \ 8 \\ \hline \end{array}$	4. $\begin{array}{r} 46 \\ \times\ \ 7 \\ \hline \end{array}$	5. $\begin{array}{r} 31 \\ \times\ \ 7 \\ \hline \end{array}$
6. $\begin{array}{r} 75 \\ \times\ \ 5 \\ \hline \end{array}$	7. $\begin{array}{r} 86 \\ \times\ \ 3 \\ \hline \end{array}$	8. $\begin{array}{r} 39 \\ \times\ \ 5 \\ \hline \end{array}$	9. $\begin{array}{r} 79 \\ \times\ \ 6 \\ \hline \end{array}$	10. $\begin{array}{r} 47 \\ \times\ \ 3 \\ \hline \end{array}$
11. $\begin{array}{r} 49 \\ \times\ \ 4 \\ \hline \end{array}$	12. $\begin{array}{r} 21 \\ \times\ \ 8 \\ \hline \end{array}$	13. $\begin{array}{r} 45 \\ \times\ \ 9 \\ \hline \end{array}$	14. $\begin{array}{r} 71 \\ \times\ \ 8 \\ \hline \end{array}$	15. $\begin{array}{r} 85 \\ \times\ \ 9 \\ \hline \end{array}$
16. $\begin{array}{r} 42 \\ \times\ \ 5 \\ \hline \end{array}$	17. $\begin{array}{r} 79 \\ \times\ \ 9 \\ \hline \end{array}$	18. $\begin{array}{r} 88 \\ \times\ \ 8 \\ \hline \end{array}$	19. $\begin{array}{r} 63 \\ \times\ \ 7 \\ \hline \end{array}$	20. $\begin{array}{r} 84 \\ \times\ \ 6 \\ \hline \end{array}$
21. $\begin{array}{r} 33 \\ \times\ \ 8 \\ \hline \end{array}$	22. $\begin{array}{r} 90 \\ \times\ \ 7 \\ \hline \end{array}$	23. $\begin{array}{r} 76 \\ \times\ \ 8 \\ \hline \end{array}$	24. $\begin{array}{r} 82 \\ \times\ \ 3 \\ \hline \end{array}$	25. $\begin{array}{r} 11 \\ \times\ \ 9 \\ \hline \end{array}$

<table><tr><td>Name:</td><td></td><td>Date: / /</td></tr><tr><td>Marks:</td><td>TIMED TEST</td><td>Time:</td></tr></table>

TIMED TEST

1.	2.	3.	4.	5.
57 × 9	36 × 2	72 × 7	93 × 2	89 × 9

6.	7.	8.	9.	10.
96 × 8	61 × 3	95 × 7	37 × 5	50 × 3

11.	12.	13.	14.	15.
67 × 8	53 × 4	59 × 4	19 × 6	12 × 4

16.	17.	18.	19.	20.
87 × 8	42 × 8	66 × 4	49 × 6	77 × 7

21.	22.	23.	24.	25.
80 × 5	29 × 5	62 × 3	88 × 6	55 × 5

24

Marks obtained:

Comment:

Name: Date: /   /

Marks:

TIMED TEST

Time:

1. 43×3	2. 91×8	3. 62×9	4. 47×3	5. 51×4
6. 63×8	7. 80×4	8. 69×8	9. 84×9	10. 27×2
11. 29×5	12. 24×8	13. 34×8	14. 22×2	15. 19×5
16. 78×2	17. 94×4	18. 23×7	19. 75×9	20. 78×8
21. 47×9	22. 66×8	23. 65×6	24. 83×7	25. 87×6

Marks obtained:

Comment:

25

TIMED TEST

1. $\begin{array}{r} 13 \\ \times \; 4 \\ \hline \end{array}$

2. $\begin{array}{r} 12 \\ \times \; 5 \\ \hline \end{array}$

3. $\begin{array}{r} 79 \\ \times \; 7 \\ \hline \end{array}$

4. $\begin{array}{r} 57 \\ \times \; 8 \\ \hline \end{array}$

5. $\begin{array}{r} 17 \\ \times \; 8 \\ \hline \end{array}$

6. $\begin{array}{r} 58 \\ \times \; 5 \\ \hline \end{array}$

7. $\begin{array}{r} 83 \\ \times \; 5 \\ \hline \end{array}$

8. $\begin{array}{r} 64 \\ \times \; 7 \\ \hline \end{array}$

9. $\begin{array}{r} 98 \\ \times \; 2 \\ \hline \end{array}$

10. $\begin{array}{r} 82 \\ \times \; 4 \\ \hline \end{array}$

11. $\begin{array}{r} 83 \\ \times \; 9 \\ \hline \end{array}$

12. $\begin{array}{r} 74 \\ \times \; 2 \\ \hline \end{array}$

13. $\begin{array}{r} 97 \\ \times \; 8 \\ \hline \end{array}$

14. $\begin{array}{r} 64 \\ \times \; 5 \\ \hline \end{array}$

15. $\begin{array}{r} 59 \\ \times \; 9 \\ \hline \end{array}$

16. $\begin{array}{r} 36 \\ \times \; 8 \\ \hline \end{array}$

17. $\begin{array}{r} 24 \\ \times \; 4 \\ \hline \end{array}$

18. $\begin{array}{r} 28 \\ \times \; 8 \\ \hline \end{array}$

19. $\begin{array}{r} 58 \\ \times \; 6 \\ \hline \end{array}$

20. $\begin{array}{r} 95 \\ \times \; 8 \\ \hline \end{array}$

21. $\begin{array}{r} 64 \\ \times \; 3 \\ \hline \end{array}$

22. $\begin{array}{r} 81 \\ \times \; 5 \\ \hline \end{array}$

23. $\begin{array}{r} 33 \\ \times \; 4 \\ \hline \end{array}$

24. $\begin{array}{r} 26 \\ \times \; 7 \\ \hline \end{array}$

25. $\begin{array}{r} 46 \\ \times \; 3 \\ \hline \end{array}$

Marks obtained: Comment:

TIMED TEST

1.
$$91 \times 5$$

2.
$$98 \times 8$$

3.
$$94 \times 5$$

4.
$$83 \times 4$$

5.
$$38 \times 3$$

6.
$$81 \times 2$$

7.
$$16 \times 4$$

8.
$$74 \times 6$$

9.
$$26 \times 4$$

10.
$$85 \times 9$$

11.
$$25 \times 8$$

12.
$$85 \times 8$$

13.
$$92 \times 3$$

14.
$$87 \times 9$$

15.
$$96 \times 7$$

16.
$$21 \times 4$$

17.
$$53 \times 4$$

18.
$$28 \times 2$$

19.
$$99 \times 4$$

20.
$$90 \times 8$$

21.
$$49 \times 3$$

22.
$$35 \times 2$$

23.
$$44 \times 5$$

24.
$$25 \times 5$$

25.
$$32 \times 9$$

TIMED TEST

1.
$$83 \times 7$$

2.
$$95 \times 8$$

3.
$$78 \times 9$$

4.
$$72 \times 5$$

5.
$$49 \times 9$$

6.
$$37 \times 8$$

7.
$$70 \times 6$$

8.
$$35 \times 8$$

9.
$$81 \times 3$$

10.
$$73 \times 2$$

11.
$$14 \times 3$$

12.
$$22 \times 9$$

13.
$$64 \times 5$$

14.
$$77 \times 4$$

15.
$$39 \times 5$$

16.
$$21 \times 5$$

17.
$$67 \times 9$$

18.
$$51 \times 4$$

19.
$$71 \times 7$$

20.
$$42 \times 5$$

21.
$$32 \times 5$$

22.
$$16 \times 8$$

23.
$$61 \times 3$$

24.
$$65 \times 6$$

25.
$$53 \times 3$$

Marks obtained: Comment:

Name:		Date: / /
Marks:	**TIMED TEST**	Time:

1. $\begin{array}{r} 53 \\ \times\ 3 \\ \hline \end{array}$	2. $\begin{array}{r} 42 \\ \times\ 7 \\ \hline \end{array}$	3. $\begin{array}{r} 44 \\ \times\ 7 \\ \hline \end{array}$	4. $\begin{array}{r} 28 \\ \times\ 4 \\ \hline \end{array}$	5. $\begin{array}{r} 39 \\ \times\ 6 \\ \hline \end{array}$
6. $\begin{array}{r} 93 \\ \times\ 7 \\ \hline \end{array}$	7. $\begin{array}{r} 65 \\ \times\ 7 \\ \hline \end{array}$	8. $\begin{array}{r} 40 \\ \times\ 7 \\ \hline \end{array}$	9. $\begin{array}{r} 25 \\ \times\ 8 \\ \hline \end{array}$	10. $\begin{array}{r} 65 \\ \times\ 9 \\ \hline \end{array}$
11. $\begin{array}{r} 15 \\ \times\ 2 \\ \hline \end{array}$	12. $\begin{array}{r} 17 \\ \times\ 6 \\ \hline \end{array}$	13. $\begin{array}{r} 86 \\ \times\ 4 \\ \hline \end{array}$	14. $\begin{array}{r} 76 \\ \times\ 5 \\ \hline \end{array}$	15. $\begin{array}{r} 59 \\ \times\ 3 \\ \hline \end{array}$
16. $\begin{array}{r} 27 \\ \times\ 4 \\ \hline \end{array}$	17. $\begin{array}{r} 83 \\ \times\ 8 \\ \hline \end{array}$	18. $\begin{array}{r} 54 \\ \times\ 3 \\ \hline \end{array}$	19. $\begin{array}{r} 43 \\ \times\ 5 \\ \hline \end{array}$	20. $\begin{array}{r} 49 \\ \times\ 4 \\ \hline \end{array}$
21. $\begin{array}{r} 38 \\ \times\ 5 \\ \hline \end{array}$	22. $\begin{array}{r} 82 \\ \times\ 7 \\ \hline \end{array}$	23. $\begin{array}{r} 63 \\ \times\ 6 \\ \hline \end{array}$	24. $\begin{array}{r} 16 \\ \times\ 9 \\ \hline \end{array}$	25. $\begin{array}{r} 52 \\ \times\ 7 \\ \hline \end{array}$

Marks obtained:

Comment:

29

TIMED TEST

1. 18×4	2. 87×2	3. 80×5
4. 92×9	5. 39×3	

1.   18 × 4
2.   87 × 2
3.   80 × 5
4.   92 × 9
5.   39 × 3
6.   48 × 8
7.   31 × 7
8.   71 × 5
9.   63 × 4
10.   52 × 8
11.   89 × 7
12.   66 × 9
13.   31 × 6
14.   51 × 7
15.   47 × 9
16.   22 × 3
17.   62 × 5
18.   59 × 3
19.   32 × 3
20.   46 × 8
21.   65 × 7
22.   96 × 3
23.   41 × 6
24.   32 × 7
25.   57 × 7

Marks obtained: Comment:

30

Marks:

TIMED TEST

Time:

1. $$75 \times 6$$

2. $$15 \times 9$$

3. $$64 \times 9$$

4. $$51 \times 8$$

5. $$48 \times 6$$

6. $$74 \times 5$$

7. $$18 \times 8$$

8. $$60 \times 7$$

9. $$64 \times 6$$

10. $$72 \times 7$$

11. $$92 \times 8$$

12. $$37 \times 2$$

13. $$86 \times 3$$

14. $$26 \times 8$$

15. $$97 \times 8$$

16. $$27 \times 6$$

17. $$39 \times 2$$

18. $$56 \times 3$$

19. $$89 \times 7$$

20. $$54 \times 7$$

21. $$31 \times 6$$

22. $$12 \times 8$$

23. $$23 \times 7$$

24. $$61 \times 5$$

25. $$25 \times 5$$

Marks obtained:

Comment:

TIMED TEST

1.
$$79 \times 6$$

2.
$$55 \times 4$$

3.
$$37 \times 9$$

4.
$$57 \times 9$$

5.
$$55 \times 2$$

6.
$$63 \times 8$$

7.
$$67 \times 4$$

8.
$$47 \times 9$$

9.
$$93 \times 6$$

10.
$$82 \times 9$$

11.
$$19 \times 5$$

12.
$$77 \times 6$$

13.
$$13 \times 9$$

14.
$$42 \times 3$$

15.
$$27 \times 8$$

16.
$$21 \times 9$$

17.
$$25 \times 7$$

18.
$$72 \times 2$$

19.
$$85 \times 3$$

20.
$$42 \times 2$$

21.
$$41 \times 6$$

22.
$$61 \times 5$$

23.
$$47 \times 7$$

24.
$$67 \times 3$$

25.
$$35 \times 8$$

Marks obtained: Comment:

TIMED TEST

1. 25 × 2	2. 43 × 9	3. 69 × 2	4. 78 × 3	5. 47 × 4
6. 76 × 5	7. 83 × 8	8. 22 × 8	9. 96 × 6	10. 16 × 4
11. 68 × 6	12. 61 × 8	13. 21 × 6	14. 33 × 9	15. 86 × 9
16. 31 × 8	17. 81 × 3	18. 32 × 6	19. 19 × 7	20. 44 × 4
21. 16 × 7	22. 35 × 9	23. 63 × 2	24. 71 × 7	25. 61 × 6

1.	2.	3.	4.	5.
$\begin{array}{r} 10 \\ \times \quad 4 \\ \hline \end{array}$	$\begin{array}{r} 16 \\ \times \quad 2 \\ \hline \end{array}$	$\begin{array}{r} 39 \\ \times \quad 5 \\ \hline \end{array}$	$\begin{array}{r} 88 \\ \times \quad 5 \\ \hline \end{array}$	$\begin{array}{r} 71 \\ \times \quad 4 \\ \hline \end{array}$
6.	**7.**	**8.**	**9.**	**10.**
$\begin{array}{r} 51 \\ \times \quad 5 \\ \hline \end{array}$	$\begin{array}{r} 54 \\ \times \quad 7 \\ \hline \end{array}$	$\begin{array}{r} 48 \\ \times \quad 7 \\ \hline \end{array}$	$\begin{array}{r} 62 \\ \times \quad 3 \\ \hline \end{array}$	$\begin{array}{r} 16 \\ \times \quad 8 \\ \hline \end{array}$
11.	**12.**	**13.**	**14.**	**15.**
$\begin{array}{r} 38 \\ \times \quad 5 \\ \hline \end{array}$	$\begin{array}{r} 19 \\ \times \quad 8 \\ \hline \end{array}$	$\begin{array}{r} 89 \\ \times \quad 2 \\ \hline \end{array}$	$\begin{array}{r} 82 \\ \times \quad 6 \\ \hline \end{array}$	$\begin{array}{r} 34 \\ \times \quad 4 \\ \hline \end{array}$
16.	**17.**	**18.**	**19.**	**20.**
$\begin{array}{r} 45 \\ \times \quad 9 \\ \hline \end{array}$	$\begin{array}{r} 63 \\ \times \quad 6 \\ \hline \end{array}$	$\begin{array}{r} 35 \\ \times \quad 3 \\ \hline \end{array}$	$\begin{array}{r} 32 \\ \times \quad 5 \\ \hline \end{array}$	$\begin{array}{r} 27 \\ \times \quad 8 \\ \hline \end{array}$
21.	**22.**	**23.**	**24.**	**25.**
$\begin{array}{r} 96 \\ \times \quad 3 \\ \hline \end{array}$	$\begin{array}{r} 28 \\ \times \quad 5 \\ \hline \end{array}$	$\begin{array}{r} 81 \\ \times \quad 4 \\ \hline \end{array}$	$\begin{array}{r} 90 \\ \times \quad 8 \\ \hline \end{array}$	$\begin{array}{r} 61 \\ \times \quad 6 \\ \hline \end{array}$

34

Marks obtained: Comment:

TIMED TEST

1. 64×2

2. 78×3

3. 25×3

4. 74×4

5. 82×3

6. 30×9

7. 39×2

8. 78×4

9. 32×3

10. 43×8

11. 81×2

12. 27×5

13. 99×8

14. 48×8

15. 29×7

16. 25×9

17. 67×6

18. 95×6

19. 81×7

20. 50×9

21. 54×7

22. 28×6

23. 57×9

24. 98×8

25. 86×3

Marks obtained: Comment:

35

Name: ___________________   Date: __ / __ / __

Marks: __________   # TIMED TEST   Time: __________

1. 88 × 6	2. 86 × 6

1.   88 × 6

2.   86 × 6

3.   61 × 7

4.   89 × 8

5.   12 × 3

6.   55 × 5

7.   92 × 7

8.   32 × 8

9.   76 × 6

10.   25 × 8

11.   36 × 9

12.   92 × 8

13.   78 × 4

14.   97 × 8

15.   61 × 3

16.   34 × 6

17.   35 × 7

18.   42 × 8

19.   75 × 3

20.   76 × 7

21.   81 × 8

22.   69 × 9

23.   51 × 9

24.   27 × 2

25.   91 × 6

36

Marks obtained: __________   Comment: __________

TIMED TEST

1. 46×7

2. 67×8

3. 56×8

4. 45×9

5. 33×9

6. 28×5

7. 89×3

8. 70×8

9. 22×3

10. 54×2

11. 82×3

12. 39×4

13. 88×2

14. 51×6

15. 92×4

16. 55×6

17. 68×2

18. 10×5

19. 14×7

20. 24×7

21. 59×8

22. 91×7

23. 37×9

24. 50×9

25. 95×5

Marks: **TIMED TEST** Time:

1. 96 × 8	2. 45 × 2	3. 31 × 6	4. 57 × 9	5. 94 × 3
6. 17 × 9	7. 60 × 4	8. 75 × 6	9. 32 × 8	10. 82 × 8
11. 43 × 9	12. 47 × 6	13. 97 × 7	14. 64 × 4	15. 87 × 5
16. 15 × 8	17. 44 × 4	18. 63 × 8	19. 25 × 7	20. 84 × 8
21. 73 × 8	22. 19 × 5	23. 58 × 7	24. 36 × 6	25. 67 × 0

Marks obtained: Comment:

TIMED TEST

1. 84×7	2. 13×9	3. 48×6	4. 92×8	5. 30×8
6. 67×7	7. 98×3	8. 33×7	9. 82×7	10. 23×5
11. 90×2	12. 28×9	13. 72×3	14. 91×3	15. 59×8
16. 85×3	17. 27×7	18. 91×3	19. 46×4	20. 72×5
21. 77×9	22. 62×5	23. 94×2	24. 42×5	25. 81×7

TIMED TEST

1.
$$\begin{array}{r} 21 \\ \times\ 6 \\ \hline \end{array}$$

2.
$$\begin{array}{r} 82 \\ \times\ 3 \\ \hline \end{array}$$

3.
$$\begin{array}{r} 53 \\ \times\ 7 \\ \hline \end{array}$$

4.
$$\begin{array}{r} 33 \\ \times\ 8 \\ \hline \end{array}$$

5.
$$\begin{array}{r} 83 \\ \times\ 2 \\ \hline \end{array}$$

6.
$$\begin{array}{r} 38 \\ \times\ 8 \\ \hline \end{array}$$

7.
$$\begin{array}{r} 87 \\ \times\ 6 \\ \hline \end{array}$$

8.
$$\begin{array}{r} 35 \\ \times\ 9 \\ \hline \end{array}$$

9.
$$\begin{array}{r} 16 \\ \times\ 9 \\ \hline \end{array}$$

10.
$$\begin{array}{r} 49 \\ \times\ 8 \\ \hline \end{array}$$

11.
$$\begin{array}{r} 68 \\ \times\ 5 \\ \hline \end{array}$$

12.
$$\begin{array}{r} 17 \\ \times\ 6 \\ \hline \end{array}$$

13.
$$\begin{array}{r} 69 \\ \times\ 3 \\ \hline \end{array}$$

14.
$$\begin{array}{r} 75 \\ \times\ 8 \\ \hline \end{array}$$

15.
$$\begin{array}{r} 39 \\ \times\ 9 \\ \hline \end{array}$$

16.
$$\begin{array}{r} 18 \\ \times\ 9 \\ \hline \end{array}$$

17.
$$\begin{array}{r} 99 \\ \times\ 2 \\ \hline \end{array}$$

18.
$$\begin{array}{r} 81 \\ \times\ 8 \\ \hline \end{array}$$

19.
$$\begin{array}{r} 44 \\ \times\ 9 \\ \hline \end{array}$$

20.
$$\begin{array}{r} 57 \\ \times\ 3 \\ \hline \end{array}$$

21.
$$\begin{array}{r} 79 \\ \times\ 5 \\ \hline \end{array}$$

22.
$$\begin{array}{r} 97 \\ \times\ 6 \\ \hline \end{array}$$

23.
$$\begin{array}{r} 68 \\ \times\ 8 \\ \hline \end{array}$$

24.
$$\begin{array}{r} 92 \\ \times\ 5 \\ \hline \end{array}$$

25.
$$\begin{array}{r} 64 \\ \times\ 8 \\ \hline \end{array}$$

Marks obtained: Comment:

TIMED TEST

1. 34×7	2. 48×6	3. 29×4	4. 76×4	5. 27×7
6. 89×8	7. 65×3	8. 53×7	9. 64×6	10. 43×7
11. 84×9	12. 89×9	13. 75×9	14. 87×4	15. 82×7
16. 92×3	17. 91×2	18. 22×8	19. 58×6	20. 39×2
21. 53×3	22. 64×8	23. 96×3	24. 67×9	25. 26×7

TIMED TEST

1. $\begin{array}{r} 57 \\ \times\ \ 4 \\ \hline \end{array}$	2. $\begin{array}{r} 50 \\ \times\ \ 3 \\ \hline \end{array}$	3. $\begin{array}{r} 71 \\ \times\ \ 6 \\ \hline \end{array}$	4. $\begin{array}{r} 75 \\ \times\ \ 9 \\ \hline \end{array}$	5. $\begin{array}{r} 48 \\ \times\ \ 8 \\ \hline \end{array}$
6. $\begin{array}{r} 85 \\ \times\ \ 7 \\ \hline \end{array}$	7. $\begin{array}{r} 93 \\ \times\ \ 6 \\ \hline \end{array}$	8. $\begin{array}{r} 56 \\ \times\ \ 2 \\ \hline \end{array}$	9. $\begin{array}{r} 18 \\ \times\ \ 9 \\ \hline \end{array}$	10. $\begin{array}{r} 18 \\ \times\ \ 9 \\ \hline \end{array}$
11. $\begin{array}{r} 91 \\ \times\ \ 8 \\ \hline \end{array}$	12. $\begin{array}{r} 26 \\ \times\ \ 4 \\ \hline \end{array}$	13. $\begin{array}{r} 41 \\ \times\ \ 2 \\ \hline \end{array}$	14. $\begin{array}{r} 49 \\ \times\ \ 8 \\ \hline \end{array}$	15. $\begin{array}{r} 64 \\ \times\ \ 7 \\ \hline \end{array}$
16. $\begin{array}{r} 79 \\ \times\ \ 5 \\ \hline \end{array}$	17. $\begin{array}{r} 98 \\ \times\ \ 5 \\ \hline \end{array}$	18. $\begin{array}{r} 44 \\ \times\ \ 3 \\ \hline \end{array}$	19. $\begin{array}{r} 25 \\ \times\ \ 5 \\ \hline \end{array}$	20. $\begin{array}{r} 17 \\ \times\ \ 7 \\ \hline \end{array}$
21. $\begin{array}{r} 97 \\ \times\ \ 9 \\ \hline \end{array}$	22. $\begin{array}{r} 28 \\ \times\ \ 7 \\ \hline \end{array}$	23. $\begin{array}{r} 43 \\ \times\ \ 9 \\ \hline \end{array}$	24. $\begin{array}{r} 76 \\ \times\ \ 9 \\ \hline \end{array}$	25. $\begin{array}{r} 68 \\ \times\ \ 7 \\ \hline \end{array}$

42

Marks obtained: Comment:

TIMED TEST

1. 59×8	2. 52×9	3. 53×2	4. 42×4	5. 85×6
6. 43×8	7. 28×9	8. 29×2	9. 21×9	10. 61×3
11. 78×7	12. 81×6	13. 26×9	14. 68×3	15. 51×7
16. 99×5	17. 72×6	18. 54×7	19. 73×6	20. 86×7
21. 69×9	22. 91×9	23. 24×8	24. 62×8	25. 61×6

TIMED TEST

1.
$$62 \times 3$$

2.
$$48 \times 6$$

3.
$$27 \times 9$$

4.
$$53 \times 8$$

5.
$$83 \times 9$$

6.
$$38 \times 8$$

7.
$$34 \times 5$$

8.
$$15 \times 4$$

9.
$$97 \times 7$$

10.
$$84 \times 9$$

11.
$$92 \times 3$$

12.
$$93 \times 9$$

13.
$$99 \times 8$$

14.
$$83 \times 6$$

15.
$$72 \times 8$$

16.
$$28 \times 9$$

17.
$$64 \times 6$$

18.
$$94 \times 7$$

19.
$$68 \times 9$$

20.
$$43 \times 8$$

21.
$$95 \times 4$$

22.
$$66 \times 9$$

23.
$$49 \times 7$$

24.
$$78 \times 9$$

25.
$$88 \times 5$$

Marks obtained: Comment:

44

TIMED TEST

1. 77×2	2. 56×2	3. 69×8	4. 81×9	5. 65×6
6. 21×7	7. 39×4	8. 25×5	9. 90×8	10. 48×5
11. 66×8	12. 88×8	13. 86×6	14. 47×3	15. 16×6
16. 91×7	17. 62×5	18. 89×7	19. 96×3	20. 48×7
21. 45×8	22. 84×6	23. 82×7	24. 88×9	25. 95×3

Marks obtained: Comment:

Marks:　　　　　# TIMED TEST　　Time:

1. 98 × 7	2. 71 × 7	3. 84 × 5	4. 33 × 8	5. 15 × 7
6. 67 × 2	7. 66 × 7	8. 95 × 4	9. 11 × 9	10. 81 × 8
11. 42 × 7	12. 64 × 5	13. 74 × 4	14. 94 × 8	15. 79 × 3
16. 47 × 5	17. 59 × 5	18. 74 × 6	19. 45 × 9	20. 19 × 6
21. 74 × 6	22. 55 × 8	23. 62 × 3	24. 69 × 9	25. 90 × 6

Marks obtained:　　　　　Comment:

1. 93 × 5	2. 45 × 9	3. 86 × 5	4. 25 × 6	5. 62 × 4
6. 51 × 6	7. 91 × 7	8. 63 × 3	9. 97 × 8	10. 81 × 6
11. 48 × 2	12. 29 × 3	13. 25 × 9	14. 95 × 7	15. 42 × 9
16. 28 × 9	17. 41 × 4	18. 26 × 8	19. 57 × 8	20. 84 × 8
21. 74 × 6	22. 72 × 7	23. 93 × 5	24. 66 × 5	25. 29 × 4

Marks obtained:

Comment:

47

TIMED TEST

1.
$$48 \times 3$$

2.
$$47 \times 4$$

3.
$$72 \times 9$$

4.
$$80 \times 4$$

5.
$$91 \times 3$$

6.
$$83 \times 6$$

7.
$$57 \times 5$$

8.
$$59 \times 9$$

9.
$$65 \times 5$$

10.
$$45 \times 4$$

11.
$$78 \times 6$$

12.
$$49 \times 6$$

13.
$$38 \times 2$$

14.
$$76 \times 7$$

15.
$$17 \times 8$$

16.
$$68 \times 9$$

17.
$$57 \times 3$$

18.
$$87 \times 9$$

19.
$$69 \times 3$$

20.
$$81 \times 9$$

21.
$$90 \times 4$$

22.
$$25 \times 7$$

23.
$$98 \times 8$$

24.
$$97 \times 3$$

25.
$$88 \times 5$$

Marks obtained:

Comment:

1. $\begin{array}{r} 36 \\ \times\ 7 \\ \hline \end{array}$	**2.** $\begin{array}{r} 37 \\ \times\ 7 \\ \hline \end{array}$	**3.** $\begin{array}{r} 73 \\ \times\ 5 \\ \hline \end{array}$	**4.** $\begin{array}{r} 61 \\ \times\ 8 \\ \hline \end{array}$	**5.** $\begin{array}{r} 15 \\ \times\ 9 \\ \hline \end{array}$
6. $\begin{array}{r} 13 \\ \times\ 3 \\ \hline \end{array}$	**7.** $\begin{array}{r} 93 \\ \times\ 4 \\ \hline \end{array}$	**8.** $\begin{array}{r} 69 \\ \times\ 7 \\ \hline \end{array}$	**9.** $\begin{array}{r} 74 \\ \times\ 9 \\ \hline \end{array}$	**10.** $\begin{array}{r} 20 \\ \times\ 6 \\ \hline \end{array}$
11. $\begin{array}{r} 34 \\ \times\ 9 \\ \hline \end{array}$	**12.** $\begin{array}{r} 82 \\ \times\ 4 \\ \hline \end{array}$	**13.** $\begin{array}{r} 93 \\ \times\ 9 \\ \hline \end{array}$	**14.** $\begin{array}{r} 43 \\ \times\ 9 \\ \hline \end{array}$	**15.** $\begin{array}{r} 98 \\ \times\ 8 \\ \hline \end{array}$
16. $\begin{array}{r} 24 \\ \times\ 9 \\ \hline \end{array}$	**17.** $\begin{array}{r} 67 \\ \times\ 5 \\ \hline \end{array}$	**18.** $\begin{array}{r} 61 \\ \times\ 7 \\ \hline \end{array}$	**19.** $\begin{array}{r} 39 \\ \times\ 7 \\ \hline \end{array}$	**20.** $\begin{array}{r} 23 \\ \times\ 5 \\ \hline \end{array}$
21. $\begin{array}{r} 62 \\ \times\ 6 \\ \hline \end{array}$	**22.** $\begin{array}{r} 57 \\ \times\ 3 \\ \hline \end{array}$	**23.** $\begin{array}{r} 81 \\ \times\ 5 \\ \hline \end{array}$	**24.** $\begin{array}{r} 99 \\ \times\ 7 \\ \hline \end{array}$	**25.** $\begin{array}{r} 73 \\ \times\ 2 \\ \hline \end{array}$

Marks obtained: Comment:

49

TIMED TEST

1.	2.	3.	4.	5.
96 × 5	64 × 9	74 × 9	72 × 7	21 × 5

6.	7.	8.	9.	10.
85 × 6	43 × 2	97 × 5	24 × 3	49 × 4

11.	12.	13.	14.	15.
18 × 3	92 × 6	62 × 7	88 × 3	24 × 5

16.	17.	18.	19.	20.
73 × 5	55 × 7	76 × 5	95 × 5	79 × 6

21.	22.	23.	24.	25.
35 × 3	41 × 4	91 × 5	19 × 3	30 × 9

50

Marks obtained: ____________ Comment: ____________

Name: Date: / /

Marks: Time:

1. $\begin{array}{r} 26 \\ \times\ 29 \\ \hline \end{array}$	2. $\begin{array}{r} 86 \\ \times\ 10 \\ \hline \end{array}$	3. $\begin{array}{r} 46 \\ \times\ 21 \\ \hline \end{array}$	4. $\begin{array}{r} 25 \\ \times\ 19 \\ \hline \end{array}$	5. $\begin{array}{r} 12 \\ \times\ 81 \\ \hline \end{array}$
6. $\begin{array}{r} 80 \\ \times\ 33 \\ \hline \end{array}$	7. $\begin{array}{r} 52 \\ \times\ 29 \\ \hline \end{array}$	8. $\begin{array}{r} 17 \\ \times\ 49 \\ \hline \end{array}$	9. $\begin{array}{r} 12 \\ \times\ 76 \\ \hline \end{array}$	10. $\begin{array}{r} 22 \\ \times\ 40 \\ \hline \end{array}$
11. $\begin{array}{r} 36 \\ \times\ 20 \\ \hline \end{array}$	12. $\begin{array}{r} 19 \\ \times\ 82 \\ \hline \end{array}$	13. $\begin{array}{r} 73 \\ \times\ 47 \\ \hline \end{array}$	14. $\begin{array}{r} 34 \\ \times\ 60 \\ \hline \end{array}$	15. $\begin{array}{r} 77 \\ \times\ 13 \\ \hline \end{array}$
16. $\begin{array}{r} 10 \\ \times\ 31 \\ \hline \end{array}$	17. $\begin{array}{r} 54 \\ \times\ 14 \\ \hline \end{array}$	18. $\begin{array}{r} 71 \\ \times\ 17 \\ \hline \end{array}$	19. $\begin{array}{r} 16 \\ \times\ 28 \\ \hline \end{array}$	20. $\begin{array}{r} 26 \\ \times\ 61 \\ \hline \end{array}$

Marks obtained: Comment:

Name: _______________ Date: __ / __ / __

Marks: _______

TIMED TEST

Time: _______

1. 29 × 20	2. 49 × 35	3. 62 × 51	4. 54 × 21	5. 72 × 17

1.
$$29 \times 20$$

2.
$$49 \times 35$$

3.
$$62 \times 51$$

4.
$$54 \times 21$$

5.
$$72 \times 17$$

6.
$$53 \times 39$$

7.
$$13 \times 96$$

8.
$$44 \times 30$$

9.
$$74 \times 75$$

10.
$$78 \times 63$$

11.
$$54 \times 93$$

12.
$$79 \times 95$$

13.
$$69 \times 31$$

14.
$$81 \times 97$$

15.
$$98 \times 75$$

16.
$$37 \times 46$$

17.
$$99 \times 92$$

18.
$$77 \times 47$$

19.
$$98 \times 35$$

20.
$$74 \times 25$$

52

Marks obtained: _______

Comment: _______

TIMED TEST

1.
```
    5 6
X   8 1
________
```

2.
```
    6 8
X   9 7
________
```

3.
```
    6 3
X   8 8
________
```

4.
```
    4 7
X   3 6
________
```

5.
```
    2 7
X   6 2
________
```

6.
```
    7 7
X   6 5
________
```

7.
```
    9 1
X   3 4
________
```

8.
```
    5 9
X   4 8
________
```

9.
```
    7 9
X   6 9
________
```

10.
```
    9 7
X   2 9
________
```

11.
```
    5 4
X   4 2
________
```

12.
```
    9 9
X   4 0
________
```

13.
```
    7 8
X   4 2
________
```

14.
```
    9 3
X   8 7
________
```

15.
```
    2 4
X   4 9
________
```

16.
```
    5 2
X   3 5
________
```

17.
```
    5 3
X   8 7
________
```

18.
```
    6 4
X   7 7
________
```

19.
```
    1 9
X   7 9
________
```

20.
```
    2 7
X   6 1
________
```

Marks obtained: Comment:

53

TIMED TEST

1.   7 5   × 8 6

2.   6 9   × 3 7

3.   8 5   × 3 9

4.   9 1   × 4 5

5.   5 9   × 5 2

6.   1 7   × 2 3

7.   7 9   × 1 8

8.   2 7   × 4 1

9.   5 1   × 9 3

10.   9 2   × 5 0

11.   1 9   × 5 4

12.   6 2   × 2 4

13.   5 6   × 6 1

14.   1 5   × 6 8

15.   9 4   × 4 2

16.   9 7   × 3 8

17.   2 3   × 9 3

18.   3 2   × 8 8

19.   9 8   × 8 4

20.   9 9   × 5 8

Marks obtained: Comment:

TIMED TEST

Name: Date: /   /

Marks: Time:

1. 96 × 66	2. 67 × 16	3. 53 × 85	4. 19 × 40	5. 71 × 94
6. 25 × 74	7. 34 × 53	8. 34 × 76	9. 83 × 10	10. 29 × 65
11. 53 × 15	12. 56 × 81	13. 27 × 38	14. 90 × 84	15. 86 × 65
16. 31 × 75	17. 46 × 74	18. 57 × 79	19. 44 × 88	20. 78 × 26

Marks obtained: Comment:

55

TIMED TEST

Marks: Time:

1.
$$
\begin{array}{r}
9\ 2 \\
\times\ 9\ 9 \\
\hline
\end{array}
$$

2.
$$
\begin{array}{r}
3\ 6 \\
\times\ 8\ 8 \\
\hline
\end{array}
$$

3.
$$
\begin{array}{r}
4\ 7 \\
\times\ 4\ 1 \\
\hline
\end{array}
$$

4.
$$
\begin{array}{r}
6\ 3 \\
\times\ 5\ 0 \\
\hline
\end{array}
$$

5.
$$
\begin{array}{r}
1\ 3 \\
\times\ 2\ 9 \\
\hline
\end{array}
$$

6.
$$
\begin{array}{r}
5\ 2 \\
\times\ 1\ 7 \\
\hline
\end{array}
$$

7.
$$
\begin{array}{r}
3\ 5 \\
\times\ 2\ 9 \\
\hline
\end{array}
$$

8.
$$
\begin{array}{r}
3\ 9 \\
\times\ 7\ 4 \\
\hline
\end{array}
$$

9.
$$
\begin{array}{r}
9\ 8 \\
\times\ 6\ 6 \\
\hline
\end{array}
$$

10.
$$
\begin{array}{r}
4\ 2 \\
\times\ 1\ 4 \\
\hline
\end{array}
$$

11.
$$
\begin{array}{r}
8\ 2 \\
\times\ 7\ 5 \\
\hline
\end{array}
$$

12.
$$
\begin{array}{r}
3\ 2 \\
\times\ 5\ 1 \\
\hline
\end{array}
$$

13.
$$
\begin{array}{r}
4\ 6 \\
\times\ 5\ 1 \\
\hline
\end{array}
$$

14.
$$
\begin{array}{r}
7\ 4 \\
\times\ 1\ 2 \\
\hline
\end{array}
$$

15.
$$
\begin{array}{r}
2\ 9 \\
\times\ 2\ 7 \\
\hline
\end{array}
$$

16.
$$
\begin{array}{r}
9\ 1 \\
\times\ 6\ 7 \\
\hline
\end{array}
$$

17.
$$
\begin{array}{r}
8\ 7 \\
\times\ 3\ 6 \\
\hline
\end{array}
$$

18.
$$
\begin{array}{r}
3\ 8 \\
\times\ 1\ 3 \\
\hline
\end{array}
$$

19.
$$
\begin{array}{r}
3\ 5 \\
\times\ 4\ 1 \\
\hline
\end{array}
$$

20.
$$
\begin{array}{r}
4\ 9 \\
\times\ 2\ 6 \\
\hline
\end{array}
$$

56

Marks obtained: Comment:

1.
$$\begin{array}{r} 3\ 4 \\ \times\ 4\ 5 \\ \hline \\ \hline \end{array}$$

2.
$$\begin{array}{r} 3\ 2 \\ \times\ 9\ 1 \\ \hline \\ \hline \end{array}$$

3.
$$\begin{array}{r} 7\ 7 \\ \times\ 6\ 4 \\ \hline \\ \hline \end{array}$$

4.
$$\begin{array}{r} 4\ 5 \\ \times\ 5\ 6 \\ \hline \\ \hline \end{array}$$

5.
$$\begin{array}{r} 7\ 2 \\ \times\ 9\ 5 \\ \hline \\ \hline \end{array}$$

6.
$$\begin{array}{r} 5\ 8 \\ \times\ 4\ 7 \\ \hline \\ \hline \end{array}$$

7.
$$\begin{array}{r} 4\ 5 \\ \times\ 6\ 6 \\ \hline \\ \hline \end{array}$$

8.
$$\begin{array}{r} 2\ 2 \\ \times\ 6\ 1 \\ \hline \\ \hline \end{array}$$

9.
$$\begin{array}{r} 8\ 8 \\ \times\ 1\ 2 \\ \hline \\ \hline \end{array}$$

10.
$$\begin{array}{r} 4\ 8 \\ \times\ 3\ 1 \\ \hline \\ \hline \end{array}$$

11.
$$\begin{array}{r} 9\ 7 \\ \times\ 1\ 5 \\ \hline \\ \hline \end{array}$$

12.
$$\begin{array}{r} 9\ 1 \\ \times\ 5\ 6 \\ \hline \\ \hline \end{array}$$

13.
$$\begin{array}{r} 7\ 9 \\ \times\ 1\ 4 \\ \hline \\ \hline \end{array}$$

14.
$$\begin{array}{r} 7\ 8 \\ \times\ 8\ 5 \\ \hline \\ \hline \end{array}$$

15.
$$\begin{array}{r} 7\ 2 \\ \times\ 6\ 4 \\ \hline \\ \hline \end{array}$$

16.
$$\begin{array}{r} 3\ 7 \\ \times\ 4\ 5 \\ \hline \\ \hline \end{array}$$

17.
$$\begin{array}{r} 9\ 7 \\ \times\ 3\ 7 \\ \hline \\ \hline \end{array}$$

18.
$$\begin{array}{r} 6\ 4 \\ \times\ 6\ 9 \\ \hline \\ \hline \end{array}$$

19.
$$\begin{array}{r} 8\ 3 \\ \times\ 3\ 5 \\ \hline \\ \hline \end{array}$$

20.
$$\begin{array}{r} 9\ 9 \\ \times\ 1\ 3 \\ \hline \\ \hline \end{array}$$

Marks obtained: Comment:

57

TIMED TEST

1.	2.	3.	4.	5.
6 5 × 8 9	9 1 × 8 1	7 8 × 1 7	3 4 × 7 4	6 9 × 6 8

6.	7.	8.	9.	10.
2 7 × 4 5	7 4 × 5 9	6 7 × 3 1	7 0 × 6 2	1 6 × 9 8

11.	12.	13.	14.	15.
4 5 × 3 3	5 2 × 4 1	3 2 × 2 7	4 6 × 3 8	2 8 × 5 7

16.	17.	18.	19.	20.
6 5 × 9 9	9 4 × 4 9	2 8 × 9 4	4 1 × 8 2	1 2 × 2 7

Marks obtained:

Comment:

TIMED TEST

1.	2.	3.	4.	5.
13 × 30	83 × 70	88 × 33	81 × 69	82 × 86
6.	7.	8.	9.	10.
75 × 87	26 × 57	58 × 21	81 × 35	13 × 96
11.	12.	13.	14.	15.
29 × 59	49 × 24	64 × 45	34 × 59	43 × 38
16.	17.	18.	19.	20.
48 × 95	86 × 18	57 × 25	51 × 72	19 × 54

TIMED TEST

1.
```
    5 4
X   8 0
_______
```

2.
```
    1 2
X   1 7
_______
```

3.
```
    9 4
X   7 7
_______
```

4.
```
    8 2
X   6 8
_______
```

5.
```
    4 7
X   7 3
_______
```

6.
```
    4 6
X   5 3
_______
```

7.
```
    9 9
X   3 6
_______
```

8.
```
    5 5
X   9 2
_______
```

9.
```
    7 3
X   7 1
_______
```

10.
```
    2 5
X   3 7
_______
```

11.
```
    8 7
X   5 4
_______
```

12.
```
    8 8
X   3 4
_______
```

13.
```
    1 4
X   6 5
_______
```

14.
```
    8 5
X   5 8
_______
```

15.
```
    2 5
X   8 9
_______
```

16.
```
    8 4
X   2 5
_______
```

17.
```
    9 9
X   8 6
_______
```

18.
```
    1 9
X   5 7
_______
```

19.
```
    5 6
X   9 5
_______
```

20.
```
    9 6
X   2 7
_______
```


Marks obtained: Comment:

TIMED TEST

1. 22×78

2. 73×96

3. 40×30

4. 46×26

5. 14×66

6. 78×56

7. 54×23

8. 28×35

9. 57×17

10. 37×46

11. 25×64

12. 63×12

13. 36×55

14. 69×31

15. 55×53

16. 43×75

17. 74×32

18. 99×45

19. 49×19

20. 81×39

Marks obtained: Comment:

TIMED TEST

| 1. | 1 8 × 4 5 | 2. | 4 1 × 2 3 | 3. | 9 0 × 7 9 | 4. | 3 7 × 6 4 | 5. | 4 5 × 8 5 |

1. 18 × 45

2. 41 × 23

3. 90 × 79

4. 37 × 64

5. 45 × 85

6. 76 × 49

7. 47 × 61

8. 19 × 68

9. 55 × 81

10. 65 × 92

11. 59 × 47

12. 32 × 75

13. 72 × 21

14. 49 × 14

15. 97 × 95

16. 40 × 67

17. 17 × 93

18. 47 × 47

19. 44 × 42

20. 86 × 15

Marks obtained:

Comment:

TIMED TEST

1.
$$\begin{array}{r} 38 \\ \times\ 11 \\ \hline \\ \hline \end{array}$$

2.
$$\begin{array}{r} 12 \\ \times\ 36 \\ \hline \\ \hline \end{array}$$

3.
$$\begin{array}{r} 54 \\ \times\ 78 \\ \hline \\ \hline \end{array}$$

4.
$$\begin{array}{r} 55 \\ \times\ 16 \\ \hline \\ \hline \end{array}$$

5.
$$\begin{array}{r} 79 \\ \times\ 33 \\ \hline \\ \hline \end{array}$$

6.
$$\begin{array}{r} 34 \\ \times\ 88 \\ \hline \\ \hline \end{array}$$

7.
$$\begin{array}{r} 63 \\ \times\ 25 \\ \hline \\ \hline \end{array}$$

8.
$$\begin{array}{r} 65 \\ \times\ 21 \\ \hline \\ \hline \end{array}$$

9.
$$\begin{array}{r} 44 \\ \times\ 82 \\ \hline \\ \hline \end{array}$$

10.
$$\begin{array}{r} 51 \\ \times\ 34 \\ \hline \\ \hline \end{array}$$

11.
$$\begin{array}{r} 45 \\ \times\ 83 \\ \hline \\ \hline \end{array}$$

12.
$$\begin{array}{r} 31 \\ \times\ 49 \\ \hline \\ \hline \end{array}$$

13.
$$\begin{array}{r} 73 \\ \times\ 66 \\ \hline \\ \hline \end{array}$$

14.
$$\begin{array}{r} 49 \\ \times\ 69 \\ \hline \\ \hline \end{array}$$

15.
$$\begin{array}{r} 35 \\ \times\ 27 \\ \hline \\ \hline \end{array}$$

16.
$$\begin{array}{r} 77 \\ \times\ 52 \\ \hline \\ \hline \end{array}$$

17.
$$\begin{array}{r} 66 \\ \times\ 44 \\ \hline \\ \hline \end{array}$$

18.
$$\begin{array}{r} 72 \\ \times\ 12 \\ \hline \\ \hline \end{array}$$

19.
$$\begin{array}{r} 92 \\ \times\ 22 \\ \hline \\ \hline \end{array}$$

20.
$$\begin{array}{r} 48 \\ \times\ 28 \\ \hline \\ \hline \end{array}$$

Marks obtained: Comment:

TIMED TEST

1.	7 3 × 5 6	2.	5 8 × 9 0	3.	8 4 × 8 4	4.	6 5 × 5 7	5.	3 8 × 4 7
6.	3 4 × 3 6	7.	2 6 × 1 8	8.	4 4 × 1 4	9.	7 1 × 7 6	10.	4 6 × 8 9
11.	1 7 × 6 9	12.	2 5 × 7 5	13.	5 6 × 7 2	14.	8 4 × 3 7	15.	6 9 × 5 5
16.	7 3 × 3 3	17.	4 8 × 9 7	18.	5 2 × 9 9	19.	5 6 × 4 6	20.	2 8 × 7 5

64

Marks obtained: Comment:

TIMED TEST

1. $\begin{array}{r} 3\ 2 \\ \times\ 3\ 9 \\ \hline \end{array}$

2. $\begin{array}{r} 8\ 4 \\ \times\ 4\ 6 \\ \hline \end{array}$

3. $\begin{array}{r} 1\ 7 \\ \times\ 1\ 2 \\ \hline \end{array}$

4. $\begin{array}{r} 4\ 2 \\ \times\ 9\ 3 \\ \hline \end{array}$

5. $\begin{array}{r} 6\ 5 \\ \times\ 8\ 3 \\ \hline \end{array}$

6. $\begin{array}{r} 3\ 7 \\ \times\ 1\ 8 \\ \hline \end{array}$

7. $\begin{array}{r} 8\ 5 \\ \times\ 7\ 5 \\ \hline \end{array}$

8. $\begin{array}{r} 3\ 6 \\ \times\ 6\ 6 \\ \hline \end{array}$

9. $\begin{array}{r} 2\ 9 \\ \times\ 1\ 5 \\ \hline \end{array}$

10. $\begin{array}{r} 7\ 5 \\ \times\ 4\ 3 \\ \hline \end{array}$

11. $\begin{array}{r} 1\ 7 \\ \times\ 7\ 9 \\ \hline \end{array}$

12. $\begin{array}{r} 1\ 6 \\ \times\ 7\ 1 \\ \hline \end{array}$

13. $\begin{array}{r} 2\ 8 \\ \times\ 2\ 6 \\ \hline \end{array}$

14. $\begin{array}{r} 1\ 2 \\ \times\ 6\ 7 \\ \hline \end{array}$

15. $\begin{array}{r} 2\ 7 \\ \times\ 6\ 6 \\ \hline \end{array}$

16. $\begin{array}{r} 4\ 6 \\ \times\ 8\ 3 \\ \hline \end{array}$

17. $\begin{array}{r} 4\ 9 \\ \times\ 5\ 1 \\ \hline \end{array}$

18. $\begin{array}{r} 2\ 3 \\ \times\ 7\ 7 \\ \hline \end{array}$

19. $\begin{array}{r} 5\ 9 \\ \times\ 3\ 5 \\ \hline \end{array}$

20. $\begin{array}{r} 9\ 8 \\ \times\ 2\ 3 \\ \hline \end{array}$

TIMED TEST

1.
$$31 \times 31$$

2.
$$21 \times 34$$

3.
$$67 \times 82$$

4.
$$91 \times 63$$

5.
$$17 \times 68$$

6.
$$27 \times 89$$

7.
$$29 \times 97$$

8.
$$13 \times 78$$

9.
$$93 \times 57$$

10.
$$34 \times 82$$

11.
$$52 \times 33$$

12.
$$76 \times 82$$

13.
$$35 \times 51$$

14.
$$39 \times 54$$

15.
$$69 \times 84$$

16.
$$14 \times 56$$

17.
$$17 \times 92$$

18.
$$67 \times 53$$

19.
$$24 \times 40$$

20.
$$51 \times 91$$

Marks obtained: ______ Comment: ______

TIMED TEST

1.   88 × 59

2.   28 × 15

3.   21 × 65

4.   71 × 20

5.   87 × 74

6.   33 × 56

7.   51 × 66

8.   69 × 67

9.   39 × 15

10.   19 × 52

11.   45 × 32

12.   16 × 59

13.   44 × 72

14.   28 × 62

15.   19 × 51

16.   13 × 63

17.   62 × 28

18.   52 × 26

19.   99 × 98

20.   78 × 63

TIMED TEST

1.
```
    6 9
  × 1 2
```

2.
```
    1 9
  × 2 9
```

3.
```
    2 5
  × 7 8
```

4.
```
    2 6
  × 9 8
```

5.
```
    4 3
  × 8 1
```

6.
```
    9 6
  × 5 1
```

7.
```
    1 6
  × 4 8
```

8.
```
    1 8
  × 6 1
```

9.
```
    8 8
  × 5 6
```

10.
```
    7 7
  × 3 3
```

11.
```
    7 6
  × 3 7
```

12.
```
    2 6
  × 6 9
```

13.
```
    6 1
  × 7 4
```

14.
```
    3 8
  × 5 9
```

15.
```
    1 9
  × 3 6
```

16.
```
    1 5
  × 8 6
```

17.
```
    9 7
  × 4 9
```

18.
```
    5 7
  × 3 5
```

19.
```
    8 2
  × 7 5
```

20.
```
    4 9
  × 7 7
```


Marks obtained: Comment:

TIMED TEST

1. $\begin{array}{r} 64 \\ \times\ 89 \\ \hline \end{array}$	2. $\begin{array}{r} 11 \\ \times\ 40 \\ \hline \end{array}$	3. $\begin{array}{r} 54 \\ \times\ 13 \\ \hline \end{array}$	4. $\begin{array}{r} 86 \\ \times\ 18 \\ \hline \end{array}$	5. $\begin{array}{r} 35 \\ \times\ 39 \\ \hline \end{array}$
6. $\begin{array}{r} 88 \\ \times\ 59 \\ \hline \end{array}$	7. $\begin{array}{r} 61 \\ \times\ 85 \\ \hline \end{array}$	8. $\begin{array}{r} 15 \\ \times\ 53 \\ \hline \end{array}$	9. $\begin{array}{r} 93 \\ \times\ 25 \\ \hline \end{array}$	10. $\begin{array}{r} 17 \\ \times\ 43 \\ \hline \end{array}$
11. $\begin{array}{r} 48 \\ \times\ 31 \\ \hline \end{array}$	12. $\begin{array}{r} 27 \\ \times\ 99 \\ \hline \end{array}$	13. $\begin{array}{r} 44 \\ \times\ 35 \\ \hline \end{array}$	14. $\begin{array}{r} 94 \\ \times\ 25 \\ \hline \end{array}$	15. $\begin{array}{r} 75 \\ \times\ 26 \\ \hline \end{array}$
16. $\begin{array}{r} 57 \\ \times\ 16 \\ \hline \end{array}$	17. $\begin{array}{r} 28 \\ \times\ 75 \\ \hline \end{array}$	18. $\begin{array}{r} 88 \\ \times\ 99 \\ \hline \end{array}$	19. $\begin{array}{r} 62 \\ \times\ 23 \\ \hline \end{array}$	20. $\begin{array}{r} 97 \\ \times\ 99 \\ \hline \end{array}$

Marks obtained: Comment:

TIMED TEST

1.	2.	3.	4.	5.
37×77	61×89	40×92	31×39	35×54

6.	7.	8.	9.	10.
71×38	56×15	69×81	83×76	38×73

11.	12.	13.	14.	15.
23×68	77×29	48×72	66×94	98×57

16.	17.	18.	19.	20.
95×48	29×79	58×55	27×67	34×88

70

Marks obtained: Comment:

TIMED TEST

1.
$$\begin{array}{r} 7\ 1 \\ \times\ 5\ 2 \\ \hline \end{array}$$

2.
$$\begin{array}{r} 5\ 7 \\ \times\ 3\ 9 \\ \hline \end{array}$$

3.
$$\begin{array}{r} 9\ 6 \\ \times\ 7\ 7 \\ \hline \end{array}$$

4.
$$\begin{array}{r} 7\ 2 \\ \times\ 6\ 9 \\ \hline \end{array}$$

5.
$$\begin{array}{r} 3\ 6 \\ \times\ 8\ 8 \\ \hline \end{array}$$

6.
$$\begin{array}{r} 7\ 7 \\ \times\ 4\ 7 \\ \hline \end{array}$$

7.
$$\begin{array}{r} 7\ 1 \\ \times\ 2\ 7 \\ \hline \end{array}$$

8.
$$\begin{array}{r} 1\ 5 \\ \times\ 4\ 3 \\ \hline \end{array}$$

9.
$$\begin{array}{r} 3\ 9 \\ \times\ 9\ 4 \\ \hline \end{array}$$

10.
$$\begin{array}{r} 6\ 5 \\ \times\ 5\ 6 \\ \hline \end{array}$$

11.
$$\begin{array}{r} 7\ 8 \\ \times\ 8\ 3 \\ \hline \end{array}$$

12.
$$\begin{array}{r} 5\ 7 \\ \times\ 6\ 8 \\ \hline \end{array}$$

13.
$$\begin{array}{r} 7\ 5 \\ \times\ 3\ 2 \\ \hline \end{array}$$

14.
$$\begin{array}{r} 8\ 6 \\ \times\ 5\ 8 \\ \hline \end{array}$$

15.
$$\begin{array}{r} 4\ 8 \\ \times\ 6\ 7 \\ \hline \end{array}$$

16.
$$\begin{array}{r} 9\ 3 \\ \times\ 8\ 4 \\ \hline \end{array}$$

17.
$$\begin{array}{r} 4\ 7 \\ \times\ 3\ 9 \\ \hline \end{array}$$

18.
$$\begin{array}{r} 7\ 6 \\ \times\ 9\ 9 \\ \hline \end{array}$$

19.
$$\begin{array}{r} 9\ 8 \\ \times\ 8\ 9 \\ \hline \end{array}$$

20.
$$\begin{array}{r} 4\ 5 \\ \times\ 8\ 7 \\ \hline \end{array}$$

Marks obtained: Comment:

TIMED TEST

1.
$$63 \times 81$$

2.
$$19 \times 65$$

3.
$$18 \times 77$$

4.
$$49 \times 68$$

5.
$$76 \times 67$$

6.
$$13 \times 97$$

7.
$$74 \times 86$$

8.
$$81 \times 94$$

9.
$$47 \times 61$$

10.
$$53 \times 67$$

11.
$$62 \times 99$$

12.
$$15 \times 84$$

13.
$$65 \times 16$$

14.
$$63 \times 42$$

15.
$$89 \times 38$$

16.
$$69 \times 98$$

17.
$$68 \times 91$$

18.
$$87 \times 26$$

19.
$$35 \times 89$$

20.
$$32 \times 64$$

72

Marks obtained: Comment:

<table>
<tr><td>Name:</td><td></td><td>Date: / /</td></tr>
<tr><td>Marks:</td><td># TIMED TEST</td><td>Time:</td></tr>
</table>

1.
$$84 \times 58$$

2.
$$89 \times 89$$

3.
$$76 \times 88$$

4.
$$29 \times 95$$

5.
$$59 \times 24$$

6.
$$66 \times 57$$

7.
$$42 \times 75$$

8.
$$87 \times 43$$

9.
$$25 \times 62$$

10.
$$77 \times 92$$

11.
$$56 \times 73$$

12.
$$79 \times 26$$

13.
$$49 \times 50$$

14.
$$47 \times 31$$

15.
$$83 \times 76$$

16.
$$89 \times 32$$

17.
$$86 \times 55$$

18.
$$35 \times 13$$

19.
$$27 \times 83$$

20.
$$38 \times 63$$

Marks obtained:

Comment:

73

TIMED TEST

1. 62 × 32	2. 24 × 83	3. 97 × 23	4. 39 × 95	5. 45 × 44
6. 85 × 14	7. 47 × 76	8. 74 × 96	9. 65 × 41	10. 76 × 57
11. 63 × 28	12. 87 × 19	13. 96 × 36	14. 27 × 48	15. 21 × 81
16. 34 × 28	17. 87 × 35	18. 44 × 49	19. 85 × 35	20. 81 × 72

Marks obtained: Comment:

TIMED TEST

1.	2.	3.	4.	5.
23×56	77×48	93×22	86×18	78×10

6.	7.	8.	9.	10.
57×46	95×61	52×76	52×64	26×69

11.	12.	13.	14.	15.
89×16	59×57	55×42	77×11	60×58

16.	17.	18.	19.	20.
81×28	58×29	46×53	68×87	97×71

Marks obtained: \
Comment:

75

TIMED TEST

1.
```
    8 9
X   8 5
_______
```

2.
```
    3 2
X   5 1
_______
```

3.
```
    5 6
X   7 9
_______
```

4.
```
    2 6
X   7 4
_______
```

5.
```
    5 4
X   8 1
_______
```

6.
```
    5 5
X   4 6
_______
```

7.
```
    8 7
X   6 6
_______
```

8.
```
    3 2
X   8 7
_______
```

9.
```
    7 4
X   1 2
_______
```

10.
```
    9 1
X   4 7
_______
```

11.
```
    4 7
X   3 7
_______
```

12.
```
    4 8
X   4 8
_______
```

13.
```
    8 2
X   7 3
_______
```

14.
```
    5 9
X   7 5
_______
```

15.
```
    9 9
X   2 1
_______
```

16.
```
    7 7
X   9 7
_______
```

17.
```
    4 3
X   5 5
_______
```

18.
```
    5 3
X   2 8
_______
```

19.
```
    1 8
X   6 8
_______
```

20.
```
    9 2
X   1 7
_______
```

76

Marks obtained: Comment:

TIMED TEST

1. 89×31
2. 32×34
3. 75×19
4. 47×35
5. 29×69
6. 28×54
7. 68×27
8. 45×84
9. 55×27
10. 31×37
11. 73×87
12. 93×89
13. 49×77
14. 53×47
15. 94×98
16. 75×58
17. 97×66
18. 44×23
19. 55×29
20. 90×88

Marks: ___

TIMED TEST

Time: ___

1.
```
    4 1
×   4 5
______
```

2.
```
    6 8
×   2 2
______
```

3.
```
    3 8
×   7 6
______
```

4.
```
    8 1
×   4 2
______
```

5.
```
    3 9
×   1 5
______
```

6.
```
    5 7
×   5 6
______
```

7.
```
    3 5
×   9 8
______
```

8.
```
    6 8
×   7 1
______
```

9.
```
    9 1
×   7 2
______
```

10.
```
    8 3
×   5 1
______
```

11.
```
    5 6
×   4 8
______
```

12.
```
    2 1
×   8 7
______
```

13.
```
    2 3
×   6 9
______
```

14.
```
    5 5
×   9 1
______
```

15.
```
    3 9
×   9 1
______
```

16.
```
    7 4
×   1 9
______
```

17.
```
    5 4
×   2 6
______
```

18.
```
    4 3
×   8 2
______
```

19.
```
    4 8
×   2 7
______
```

20.
```
    5 7
×   7 4
______
```


Marks obtained: ___   Comment: ___

Marks:

TIMED TEST

Time:

1.
$$\begin{array}{r} 43 \\ \times\ 51 \\ \hline \end{array}$$

2.
$$\begin{array}{r} 74 \\ \times\ 27 \\ \hline \end{array}$$

3.
$$\begin{array}{r} 63 \\ \times\ 38 \\ \hline \end{array}$$

4.
$$\begin{array}{r} 57 \\ \times\ 82 \\ \hline \end{array}$$

5.
$$\begin{array}{r} 56 \\ \times\ 28 \\ \hline \end{array}$$

6.
$$\begin{array}{r} 83 \\ \times\ 99 \\ \hline \end{array}$$

7.
$$\begin{array}{r} 81 \\ \times\ 29 \\ \hline \end{array}$$

8.
$$\begin{array}{r} 90 \\ \times\ 93 \\ \hline \end{array}$$

9.
$$\begin{array}{r} 49 \\ \times\ 65 \\ \hline \end{array}$$

10.
$$\begin{array}{r} 47 \\ \times\ 52 \\ \hline \end{array}$$

11.
$$\begin{array}{r} 88 \\ \times\ 67 \\ \hline \end{array}$$

12.
$$\begin{array}{r} 24 \\ \times\ 62 \\ \hline \end{array}$$

13.
$$\begin{array}{r} 13 \\ \times\ 88 \\ \hline \end{array}$$

14.
$$\begin{array}{r} 23 \\ \times\ 56 \\ \hline \end{array}$$

15.
$$\begin{array}{r} 28 \\ \times\ 85 \\ \hline \end{array}$$

16.
$$\begin{array}{r} 93 \\ \times\ 34 \\ \hline \end{array}$$

17.
$$\begin{array}{r} 45 \\ \times\ 86 \\ \hline \end{array}$$

18.
$$\begin{array}{r} 59 \\ \times\ 26 \\ \hline \end{array}$$

19.
$$\begin{array}{r} 15 \\ \times\ 96 \\ \hline \end{array}$$

20.
$$\begin{array}{r} 66 \\ \times\ 49 \\ \hline \end{array}$$

Marks obtained: Comment:

<table>
<tr><td>Name:</td><td></td><td>Date: / /</td></tr>
<tr><td>Marks:</td><td>TIMED TEST</td><td>Time:</td></tr>
</table>

TIMED TEST

1. 47 × 67	2. 81 × 16
3. 66 × 38	4. 53 × 26
5. 45 × 54	6. 73 × 43
7. 40 × 96	8. 42 × 76
9. 48 × 85	10. 62 × 25
11. 62 × 44	12. 39 × 45
13. 58 × 59	14. 67 × 18
15. 78 × 25	16. 85 × 24
17. 43 × 92	18. 78 × 28
19. 58 × 27	20. 43 × 63

80

Marks obtained:

Comment:

TIMED TEST

1.   69 × 16

2.   33 × 99

3.   29 × 67

4.   79 × 88

5.   92 × 55

6.   71 × 30

7.   46 × 75

8.   98 × 56

9.   41 × 94

10.   31 × 72

11.   48 × 37

12.   74 × 14

13.   12 × 88

14.   25 × 52

15.   17 × 83

16.   55 × 29

17.   57 × 23

18.   85 × 22

19.   74 × 61

20.   53 × 92

Marks obtained: Comment:

TIMED TEST

1.
$$\begin{array}{r} 98 \\ \times\ 96 \\ \hline \\ \hline \end{array}$$

2.
$$\begin{array}{r} 93 \\ \times\ 72 \\ \hline \\ \hline \end{array}$$

3.
$$\begin{array}{r} 55 \\ \times\ 95 \\ \hline \\ \hline \end{array}$$

4.
$$\begin{array}{r} 38 \\ \times\ 48 \\ \hline \\ \hline \end{array}$$

5.
$$\begin{array}{r} 57 \\ \times\ 54 \\ \hline \\ \hline \end{array}$$

6.
$$\begin{array}{r} 64 \\ \times\ 54 \\ \hline \\ \hline \end{array}$$

7.
$$\begin{array}{r} 23 \\ \times\ 34 \\ \hline \\ \hline \end{array}$$

8.
$$\begin{array}{r} 45 \\ \times\ 26 \\ \hline \\ \hline \end{array}$$

9.
$$\begin{array}{r} 79 \\ \times\ 92 \\ \hline \\ \hline \end{array}$$

10.
$$\begin{array}{r} 98 \\ \times\ 65 \\ \hline \\ \hline \end{array}$$

11.
$$\begin{array}{r} 65 \\ \times\ 33 \\ \hline \\ \hline \end{array}$$

12.
$$\begin{array}{r} 67 \\ \times\ 15 \\ \hline \\ \hline \end{array}$$

13.
$$\begin{array}{r} 42 \\ \times\ 96 \\ \hline \\ \hline \end{array}$$

14.
$$\begin{array}{r} 73 \\ \times\ 58 \\ \hline \\ \hline \end{array}$$

15.
$$\begin{array}{r} 77 \\ \times\ 53 \\ \hline \\ \hline \end{array}$$

16.
$$\begin{array}{r} 35 \\ \times\ 81 \\ \hline \\ \hline \end{array}$$

17.
$$\begin{array}{r} 47 \\ \times\ 65 \\ \hline \\ \hline \end{array}$$

18.
$$\begin{array}{r} 71 \\ \times\ 35 \\ \hline \\ \hline \end{array}$$

19.
$$\begin{array}{r} 83 \\ \times\ 89 \\ \hline \\ \hline \end{array}$$

20.
$$\begin{array}{r} 18 \\ \times\ 47 \\ \hline \\ \hline \end{array}$$

82

Marks obtained:

Comment:

TIMED TEST

1.
$$99 \times 28$$

2.
$$63 \times 58$$

3.
$$27 \times 95$$

4.
$$26 \times 19$$

5.
$$41 \times 84$$

6.
$$28 \times 47$$

7.
$$94 \times 18$$

8.
$$99 \times 16$$

9.
$$65 \times 81$$

10.
$$27 \times 79$$

11.
$$92 \times 68$$

12.
$$26 \times 91$$

13.
$$67 \times 42$$

14.
$$93 \times 25$$

15.
$$97 \times 59$$

16.
$$92 \times 72$$

17.
$$85 \times 63$$

18.
$$73 \times 28$$

19.
$$77 \times 63$$

20.
$$84 \times 29$$

TIMED TEST

1.	2.	3.	4.	5.
78×69	23×56	59×75	47×66	48×26

6.	7.	8.	9.	10.
28×99	47×97	74×55	94×39	29×73

11.	12.	13.	14.	15.
48×71	56×73	76×29	39×86	88×16

16.	17.	18.	19.	20.
13×78	92×56	61×79	51×25	95×61

84

Marks obtained:

Comment:

TIMED TEST

1.
$$\begin{array}{r} 66 \\ \times\ 40 \\ \hline \end{array}$$

2.
$$\begin{array}{r} 75 \\ \times\ 43 \\ \hline \end{array}$$

3.
$$\begin{array}{r} 37 \\ \times\ 90 \\ \hline \end{array}$$

4.
$$\begin{array}{r} 37 \\ \times\ 64 \\ \hline \end{array}$$

5.
$$\begin{array}{r} 93 \\ \times\ 56 \\ \hline \end{array}$$

6.
$$\begin{array}{r} 72 \\ \times\ 46 \\ \hline \end{array}$$

7.
$$\begin{array}{r} 37 \\ \times\ 12 \\ \hline \end{array}$$

8.
$$\begin{array}{r} 95 \\ \times\ 78 \\ \hline \end{array}$$

9.
$$\begin{array}{r} 23 \\ \times\ 58 \\ \hline \end{array}$$

10.
$$\begin{array}{r} 34 \\ \times\ 91 \\ \hline \end{array}$$

11.
$$\begin{array}{r} 66 \\ \times\ 37 \\ \hline \end{array}$$

12.
$$\begin{array}{r} 86 \\ \times\ 54 \\ \hline \end{array}$$

13.
$$\begin{array}{r} 47 \\ \times\ 92 \\ \hline \end{array}$$

14.
$$\begin{array}{r} 73 \\ \times\ 95 \\ \hline \end{array}$$

15.
$$\begin{array}{r} 61 \\ \times\ 24 \\ \hline \end{array}$$

16.
$$\begin{array}{r} 88 \\ \times\ 57 \\ \hline \end{array}$$

17.
$$\begin{array}{r} 75 \\ \times\ 49 \\ \hline \end{array}$$

18.
$$\begin{array}{r} 16 \\ \times\ 65 \\ \hline \end{array}$$

19.
$$\begin{array}{r} 67 \\ \times\ 81 \\ \hline \end{array}$$

20.
$$\begin{array}{r} 78 \\ \times\ 54 \\ \hline \end{array}$$

Marks obtained: Comment:

TIMED TEST

1.
    2 9
× 6 2

2.
    1 8
× 9 8

3.
    9 1
× 4 8

4.
    6 8
× 8 9

5.
    9 1
× 1 9

6.
    7 8
× 4 6

7.
    1 9
× 5 1

8.
    9 3
× 2 4

9.
    2 7
× 8 1

10.
    2 9
× 4 8

11.
    9 2
× 5 1

12.
    4 3
× 1 5

13.
    4 5
× 6 9

14.
    7 4
× 4 5

15.
    9 5
× 2 2

16.
    5 5
× 4 2

17.
    9 1
× 2 8

18.
    8 2
× 8 2

19.
    8 6
× 1 4

20.
    1 9
× 8 8

86

Marks obtained: Comment:

TIMED TEST

1. $\begin{array}{r} 41 \\ \times\ 58 \\ \hline \end{array}$	**2.** $\begin{array}{r} 59 \\ \times\ 82 \\ \hline \end{array}$	**3.** $\begin{array}{r} 32 \\ \times\ 26 \\ \hline \end{array}$	**4.** $\begin{array}{r} 53 \\ \times\ 63 \\ \hline \end{array}$	**5.** $\begin{array}{r} 62 \\ \times\ 28 \\ \hline \end{array}$
6. $\begin{array}{r} 17 \\ \times\ 75 \\ \hline \end{array}$	**7.** $\begin{array}{r} 93 \\ \times\ 17 \\ \hline \end{array}$	**8.** $\begin{array}{r} 75 \\ \times\ 18 \\ \hline \end{array}$	**9.** $\begin{array}{r} 83 \\ \times\ 16 \\ \hline \end{array}$	**10.** $\begin{array}{r} 62 \\ \times\ 43 \\ \hline \end{array}$
11. $\begin{array}{r} 48 \\ \times\ 11 \\ \hline \end{array}$	**12.** $\begin{array}{r} 47 \\ \times\ 37 \\ \hline \end{array}$	**13.** $\begin{array}{r} 57 \\ \times\ 91 \\ \hline \end{array}$	**14.** $\begin{array}{r} 15 \\ \times\ 92 \\ \hline \end{array}$	**15.** $\begin{array}{r} 17 \\ \times\ 23 \\ \hline \end{array}$
16. $\begin{array}{r} 52 \\ \times\ 29 \\ \hline \end{array}$	**17.** $\begin{array}{r} 97 \\ \times\ 83 \\ \hline \end{array}$	**18.** $\begin{array}{r} 81 \\ \times\ 73 \\ \hline \end{array}$	**19.** $\begin{array}{r} 47 \\ \times\ 39 \\ \hline \end{array}$	**20.** $\begin{array}{r} 49 \\ \times\ 95 \\ \hline \end{array}$

Marks obtained: **Comment:**

Marks: # TIMED TEST   Time:

1.	2.	3.	4.	5.
$\begin{array}{r} 13 \\ \times\ 56 \\ \hline \end{array}$	$\begin{array}{r} 55 \\ \times\ 52 \\ \hline \end{array}$	$\begin{array}{r} 28 \\ \times\ 44 \\ \hline \end{array}$	$\begin{array}{r} 17 \\ \times\ 98 \\ \hline \end{array}$	$\begin{array}{r} 64 \\ \times\ 36 \\ \hline \end{array}$
6.	7.	8.	9.	10.
$\begin{array}{r} 75 \\ \times\ 21 \\ \hline \end{array}$	$\begin{array}{r} 68 \\ \times\ 91 \\ \hline \end{array}$	$\begin{array}{r} 64 \\ \times\ 73 \\ \hline \end{array}$	$\begin{array}{r} 79 \\ \times\ 51 \\ \hline \end{array}$	$\begin{array}{r} 63 \\ \times\ 34 \\ \hline \end{array}$
11.	12.	13.	14.	15.
$\begin{array}{r} 54 \\ \times\ 63 \\ \hline \end{array}$	$\begin{array}{r} 41 \\ \times\ 49 \\ \hline \end{array}$	$\begin{array}{r} 83 \\ \times\ 61 \\ \hline \end{array}$	$\begin{array}{r} 91 \\ \times\ 42 \\ \hline \end{array}$	$\begin{array}{r} 39 \\ \times\ 93 \\ \hline \end{array}$
16.	17.	18.	19.	20.
$\begin{array}{r} 78 \\ \times\ 16 \\ \hline \end{array}$	$\begin{array}{r} 52 \\ \times\ 28 \\ \hline \end{array}$	$\begin{array}{r} 29 \\ \times\ 88 \\ \hline \end{array}$	$\begin{array}{r} 52 \\ \times\ 65 \\ \hline \end{array}$	$\begin{array}{r} 67 \\ \times\ 14 \\ \hline \end{array}$

88

Marks obtained: Comment:

TIMED TEST

1.
$$\begin{array}{r} 7\ 3 \\ \times\ 9\ 7 \\ \hline \end{array}$$

2.
$$\begin{array}{r} 1\ 4 \\ \times\ 3\ 5 \\ \hline \end{array}$$

3.
$$\begin{array}{r} 7\ 4 \\ \times\ 9\ 6 \\ \hline \end{array}$$

4.
$$\begin{array}{r} 3\ 5 \\ \times\ 5\ 9 \\ \hline \end{array}$$

5.
$$\begin{array}{r} 4\ 3 \\ \times\ 7\ 2 \\ \hline \end{array}$$

6.
$$\begin{array}{r} 7\ 6 \\ \times\ 8\ 5 \\ \hline \end{array}$$

7.
$$\begin{array}{r} 4\ 5 \\ \times\ 2\ 8 \\ \hline \end{array}$$

8.
$$\begin{array}{r} 6\ 7 \\ \times\ 4\ 1 \\ \hline \end{array}$$

9.
$$\begin{array}{r} 4\ 5 \\ \times\ 6\ 1 \\ \hline \end{array}$$

10.
$$\begin{array}{r} 4\ 0 \\ \times\ 8\ 9 \\ \hline \end{array}$$

11.
$$\begin{array}{r} 1\ 4 \\ \times\ 9\ 7 \\ \hline \end{array}$$

12.
$$\begin{array}{r} 9\ 2 \\ \times\ 8\ 4 \\ \hline \end{array}$$

13.
$$\begin{array}{r} 6\ 8 \\ \times\ 1\ 2 \\ \hline \end{array}$$

14.
$$\begin{array}{r} 6\ 9 \\ \times\ 8\ 5 \\ \hline \end{array}$$

15.
$$\begin{array}{r} 4\ 2 \\ \times\ 4\ 9 \\ \hline \end{array}$$

16.
$$\begin{array}{r} 2\ 8 \\ \times\ 6\ 6 \\ \hline \end{array}$$

17.
$$\begin{array}{r} 4\ 3 \\ \times\ 7\ 7 \\ \hline \end{array}$$

18.
$$\begin{array}{r} 6\ 8 \\ \times\ 3\ 6 \\ \hline \end{array}$$

19.
$$\begin{array}{r} 4\ 1 \\ \times\ 7\ 8 \\ \hline \end{array}$$

20.
$$\begin{array}{r} 7\ 3 \\ \times\ 5\ 2 \\ \hline \end{array}$$

Marks obtained: Comment:

89

TIMED TEST

1.
$$\begin{array}{r} 6\ 7 \\ \times\ 1\ 2 \\ \hline \end{array}$$

2.
$$\begin{array}{r} 4\ 7 \\ \times\ 5\ 7 \\ \hline \end{array}$$

3.
$$\begin{array}{r} 3\ 2 \\ \times\ 4\ 0 \\ \hline \end{array}$$

4.
$$\begin{array}{r} 2\ 4 \\ \times\ 8\ 8 \\ \hline \end{array}$$

5.
$$\begin{array}{r} 6\ 5 \\ \times\ 5\ 1 \\ \hline \end{array}$$

6.
$$\begin{array}{r} 5\ 8 \\ \times\ 8\ 7 \\ \hline \end{array}$$

7.
$$\begin{array}{r} 4\ 7 \\ \times\ 4\ 1 \\ \hline \end{array}$$

8.
$$\begin{array}{r} 5\ 2 \\ \times\ 6\ 6 \\ \hline \end{array}$$

9.
$$\begin{array}{r} 3\ 8 \\ \times\ 2\ 7 \\ \hline \end{array}$$

10.
$$\begin{array}{r} 9\ 6 \\ \times\ 7\ 6 \\ \hline \end{array}$$

11.
$$\begin{array}{r} 9\ 5 \\ \times\ 1\ 7 \\ \hline \end{array}$$

12.
$$\begin{array}{r} 1\ 9 \\ \times\ 9\ 4 \\ \hline \end{array}$$

13.
$$\begin{array}{r} 4\ 4 \\ \times\ 9\ 3 \\ \hline \end{array}$$

14.
$$\begin{array}{r} 6\ 9 \\ \times\ 5\ 4 \\ \hline \end{array}$$

15.
$$\begin{array}{r} 6\ 5 \\ \times\ 8\ 3 \\ \hline \end{array}$$

16.
$$\begin{array}{r} 6\ 8 \\ \times\ 5\ 2 \\ \hline \end{array}$$

17.
$$\begin{array}{r} 6\ 3 \\ \times\ 4\ 8 \\ \hline \end{array}$$

18.
$$\begin{array}{r} 5\ 2 \\ \times\ 6\ 1 \\ \hline \end{array}$$

19.
$$\begin{array}{r} 9\ 3 \\ \times\ 3\ 6 \\ \hline \end{array}$$

20.
$$\begin{array}{r} 7\ 1 \\ \times\ 9\ 3 \\ \hline \end{array}$$

90

Marks obtained: Comment:

TIMED TEST

1.
$$\begin{array}{r} 46 \\ \times\ 62 \\ \hline \end{array}$$

2.
$$\begin{array}{r} 77 \\ \times\ 91 \\ \hline \end{array}$$

3.
$$\begin{array}{r} 72 \\ \times\ 65 \\ \hline \end{array}$$

4.
$$\begin{array}{r} 36 \\ \times\ 54 \\ \hline \end{array}$$

5.
$$\begin{array}{r} 60 \\ \times\ 67 \\ \hline \end{array}$$

6.
$$\begin{array}{r} 72 \\ \times\ 97 \\ \hline \end{array}$$

7.
$$\begin{array}{r} 99 \\ \times\ 48 \\ \hline \end{array}$$

8.
$$\begin{array}{r} 25 \\ \times\ 31 \\ \hline \end{array}$$

9.
$$\begin{array}{r} 33 \\ \times\ 63 \\ \hline \end{array}$$

10.
$$\begin{array}{r} 53 \\ \times\ 52 \\ \hline \end{array}$$

11.
$$\begin{array}{r} 43 \\ \times\ 78 \\ \hline \end{array}$$

12.
$$\begin{array}{r} 69 \\ \times\ 79 \\ \hline \end{array}$$

13.
$$\begin{array}{r} 32 \\ \times\ 95 \\ \hline \end{array}$$

14.
$$\begin{array}{r} 45 \\ \times\ 81 \\ \hline \end{array}$$

15.
$$\begin{array}{r} 37 \\ \times\ 86 \\ \hline \end{array}$$

16.
$$\begin{array}{r} 49 \\ \times\ 72 \\ \hline \end{array}$$

17.
$$\begin{array}{r} 48 \\ \times\ 75 \\ \hline \end{array}$$

18.
$$\begin{array}{r} 31 \\ \times\ 67 \\ \hline \end{array}$$

19.
$$\begin{array}{r} 62 \\ \times\ 54 \\ \hline \end{array}$$

20.
$$\begin{array}{r} 35 \\ \times\ 72 \\ \hline \end{array}$$

Marks obtained: Comment:

Marks: ______   # TIMED TEST   Time: ______

1. 58 × 77	**2.** 56 × 54	**3.** 85 × 47	**4.** 62 × 76	**5.** 75 × 35
6. 23 × 42	**7.** 57 × 19	**8.** 48 × 58	**9.** 88 × 32	**10.** 53 × 95
11. 34 × 57	**12.** 25 × 72	**13.** 78 × 17	**14.** 96 × 22	**15.** 33 × 67
16. 71 × 95	**17.** 59 × 76	**18.** 35 × 84	**19.** 95 × 95	**20.** 91 × 51

92

Marks obtained: ______   Comment: ______

Marks: __________   **TIMED TEST**   Time: __________

1. $\begin{array}{r} 17 \\ \times\ 45 \\ \hline \end{array}$	**2.** $\begin{array}{r} 85 \\ \times\ 97 \\ \hline \end{array}$

1. 17×45
2. 85×97
3. 65×42
4. 37×87
5. 86×91
6. 41×62
7. 88×79
8. 63×29
9. 66×66
10. 96×53
11. 35×83
12. 87×78
13. 46×29
14. 52×74
15. 64×17
16. 87×64
17. 46×39
18. 38×94
19. 71×63
20. 42×47

Marks obtained: __________   **Comment:** __________

Name:

Date: / /

Marks:

TIMED TEST

Time:

1.	2.	3.	4.	5.
2 1 × 6 9	6 7 × 5 4	8 7 × 2 5	3 3 × 9 3	1 3 × 8 1

6.	7.	8.	9.	10.
5 4 × 6 9	2 9 × 8 8	4 1 × 5 8	9 5 × 8 9	2 6 × 8 6

11.	12.	13.	14.	15.
5 7 × 9 6	7 6 × 5 5	9 2 × 1 8	2 8 × 5 3	3 7 × 9 9

16.	17.	18.	19.	20.
7 7 × 3 2	6 5 × 1 7	7 7 × 4 3	5 8 × 2 9	5 3 × 7 9

94

Marks obtained:

Comment:

TIMED TEST

1.
$$35 \times 77$$

2.
$$35 \times 28$$

3.
$$66 \times 88$$

4.
$$25 \times 94$$

5.
$$77 \times 44$$

6.
$$56 \times 81$$

7.
$$78 \times 54$$

8.
$$63 \times 42$$

9.
$$87 \times 12$$

10.
$$72 \times 81$$

11.
$$34 \times 47$$

12.
$$75 \times 29$$

13.
$$99 \times 76$$

14.
$$76 \times 62$$

15.
$$50 \times 85$$

16.
$$49 \times 33$$

17.
$$69 \times 48$$

18.
$$95 \times 41$$

19.
$$18 \times 74$$

20.
$$53 \times 83$$

Marks obtained: Comment:

TIMED TEST

1. 10 × 28	**2.** 35 × 85	**3.** 74 × 97	**4.** 49 × 19	**5.** 92 × 35
6. 79 × 88	**7.** 67 × 62	**8.** 55 × 98	**9.** 48 × 23	**10.** 87 × 69
11. 26 × 77	**12.** 74 × 28	**13.** 86 × 38	**14.** 65 × 97	**15.** 70 × 66
16. 43 × 92	**17.** 86 × 29	**18.** 82 × 93	**19.** 95 × 48	**20.** 26 × 67

Marks obtained:

Comment:

TIMED TEST

1.
```
    8 5
X   6 0
―――――
```

2.
```
    4 1
X   8 4
―――――
```

3.
```
    8 8
X   1 7
―――――
```

4.
```
    4 2
X   5 9
―――――
```

5.
```
    6 1
X   4 9
―――――
```

6.
```
    2 4
X   2 6
―――――
```

7.
```
    8 5
X   2 4
―――――
```

8.
```
    4 1
X   3 6
―――――
```

9.
```
    7 1
X   3 7
―――――
```

10.
```
    7 6
X   3 3
―――――
```

11.
```
    7 8
X   8 1
―――――
```

12.
```
    3 9
X   7 2
―――――
```

13.
```
    3 7
X   9 3
―――――
```

14.
```
    4 3
X   3 7
―――――
```

15.
```
    8 6
X   5 1
―――――
```

16.
```
    9 9
X   4 4
―――――
```

17.
```
    4 0
X   4 8
―――――
```

18.
```
    9 6
X   9 7
―――――
```

19.
```
    4 7
X   8 7
―――――
```

20.
```
    9 5
X   8 7
―――――
```

Marks obtained: Comment:

TIMED TEST

1. 18×98	2. 69×46

1.
$$\begin{array}{r} 1\ 8 \\ \times\ 9\ 8 \\ \hline \\ \hline \end{array}$$

2.
$$\begin{array}{r} 6\ 9 \\ \times\ 4\ 6 \\ \hline \\ \hline \end{array}$$

3.
$$\begin{array}{r} 2\ 8 \\ \times\ 7\ 2 \\ \hline \\ \hline \end{array}$$

4.
$$\begin{array}{r} 1\ 3 \\ \times\ 9\ 5 \\ \hline \\ \hline \end{array}$$

5.
$$\begin{array}{r} 8\ 3 \\ \times\ 4\ 6 \\ \hline \\ \hline \end{array}$$

6.
$$\begin{array}{r} 5\ 9 \\ \times\ 7\ 2 \\ \hline \\ \hline \end{array}$$

7.
$$\begin{array}{r} 4\ 7 \\ \times\ 6\ 2 \\ \hline \\ \hline \end{array}$$

8.
$$\begin{array}{r} 6\ 7 \\ \times\ 8\ 6 \\ \hline \\ \hline \end{array}$$

9.
$$\begin{array}{r} 8\ 1 \\ \times\ 1\ 2 \\ \hline \\ \hline \end{array}$$

10.
$$\begin{array}{r} 9\ 8 \\ \times\ 3\ 1 \\ \hline \\ \hline \end{array}$$

11.
$$\begin{array}{r} 8\ 6 \\ \times\ 8\ 0 \\ \hline \\ \hline \end{array}$$

12.
$$\begin{array}{r} 4\ 4 \\ \times\ 6\ 5 \\ \hline \\ \hline \end{array}$$

13.
$$\begin{array}{r} 8\ 8 \\ \times\ 9\ 2 \\ \hline \\ \hline \end{array}$$

14.
$$\begin{array}{r} 3\ 9 \\ \times\ 1\ 3 \\ \hline \\ \hline \end{array}$$

15.
$$\begin{array}{r} 6\ 2 \\ \times\ 2\ 4 \\ \hline \\ \hline \end{array}$$

16.
$$\begin{array}{r} 6\ 8 \\ \times\ 3\ 8 \\ \hline \\ \hline \end{array}$$

17.
$$\begin{array}{r} 8\ 9 \\ \times\ 2\ 9 \\ \hline \\ \hline \end{array}$$

18.
$$\begin{array}{r} 7\ 4 \\ \times\ 9\ 1 \\ \hline \\ \hline \end{array}$$

19.
$$\begin{array}{r} 4\ 8 \\ \times\ 2\ 3 \\ \hline \\ \hline \end{array}$$

20.
$$\begin{array}{r} 6\ 8 \\ \times\ 9\ 6 \\ \hline \\ \hline \end{array}$$

Marks obtained: _____ Comment: _____

<table>
<tr><td>Name:</td><td></td><td>Date: / /</td></tr>
<tr><td>Marks:</td><td>**TIMED TEST**</td><td>Time:</td></tr>
</table>

1.
```
   8 1
 × 2 6
───────
```

2.
```
   2 2
 × 6 7
───────
```

3.
```
   6 8
 × 4 2
───────
```

4.
```
   8 1
 × 1 2
───────
```

5.
```
   6 8
 × 3 3
───────
```

6.
```
   5 7
 × 8 8
───────
```

7.
```
   5 1
 × 4 1
───────
```

8.
```
   3 5
 × 7 8
───────
```

9.
```
   9 5
 × 1 9
───────
```

10.
```
   3 1
 × 7 9
───────
```

11.
```
   8 3
 × 8 7
───────
```

12.
```
   2 7
 × 9 3
───────
```

13.
```
   6 6
 × 4 9
───────
```

14.
```
   5 3
 × 9 9
───────
```

15.
```
   6 6
 × 4 8
───────
```

16.
```
   8 1
 × 3 0
───────
```

17.
```
   9 0
 × 1 0
───────
```

18.
```
   4 8
 × 1 5
───────
```

19.
```
   9 6
 × 3 9
───────
```

20.
```
   4 5
 × 9 1
───────
```

Marks obtained:

Comment:

99

TIMED TEST

1.
$$\begin{array}{r} 35 \\ \times\ 79 \\ \hline \\ \hline \end{array}$$

2.
$$\begin{array}{r} 42 \\ \times\ 75 \\ \hline \\ \hline \end{array}$$

3.
$$\begin{array}{r} 81 \\ \times\ 34 \\ \hline \\ \hline \end{array}$$

4.
$$\begin{array}{r} 56 \\ \times\ 73 \\ \hline \\ \hline \end{array}$$

5.
$$\begin{array}{r} 19 \\ \times\ 65 \\ \hline \\ \hline \end{array}$$

6.
$$\begin{array}{r} 56 \\ \times\ 78 \\ \hline \\ \hline \end{array}$$

7.
$$\begin{array}{r} 81 \\ \times\ 44 \\ \hline \\ \hline \end{array}$$

8.
$$\begin{array}{r} 34 \\ \times\ 41 \\ \hline \\ \hline \end{array}$$

9.
$$\begin{array}{r} 54 \\ \times\ 38 \\ \hline \\ \hline \end{array}$$

10.
$$\begin{array}{r} 92 \\ \times\ 13 \\ \hline \\ \hline \end{array}$$

11.
$$\begin{array}{r} 53 \\ \times\ 89 \\ \hline \\ \hline \end{array}$$

12.
$$\begin{array}{r} 31 \\ \times\ 29 \\ \hline \\ \hline \end{array}$$

13.
$$\begin{array}{r} 32 \\ \times\ 73 \\ \hline \\ \hline \end{array}$$

14.
$$\begin{array}{r} 82 \\ \times\ 21 \\ \hline \\ \hline \end{array}$$

15.
$$\begin{array}{r} 49 \\ \times\ 78 \\ \hline \\ \hline \end{array}$$

16.
$$\begin{array}{r} 55 \\ \times\ 39 \\ \hline \\ \hline \end{array}$$

17.
$$\begin{array}{r} 37 \\ \times\ 98 \\ \hline \\ \hline \end{array}$$

18.
$$\begin{array}{r} 79 \\ \times\ 74 \\ \hline \\ \hline \end{array}$$

19.
$$\begin{array}{r} 43 \\ \times\ 85 \\ \hline \\ \hline \end{array}$$

20.
$$\begin{array}{r} 88 \\ \times\ 64 \\ \hline \\ \hline \end{array}$$

100

Marks obtained: Comment:

TIMED TEST

1.
```
    4 5
X   5 6
_______
```

2.
```
    6 6
X   8 3
_______
```

3.
```
    2 6
X   7 9
_______
```

4.
```
    1 4
X   6 1
_______
```

5.
```
    6 4
X   9 0
_______
```

6.
```
    5 3
X   1 5
_______
```

7.
```
    1 4
X   6 7
_______
```

8.
```
    6 2
X   5 3
_______
```

9.
```
    8 1
X   2 7
_______
```

10.
```
    4 2
X   3 8
_______
```

11.
```
    5 3
X   6 2
_______
```

12.
```
    2 8
X   5 9
_______
```

13.
```
    9 7
X   7 1
_______
```

14.
```
    9 4
X   3 3
_______
```

15.
```
    5 4
X   5 3
_______
```

16.
```
    6 2
X   1 8
_______
```

17.
```
    7 2
X   9 6
_______
```

18.
```
    6 9
X   2 2
_______
```

19.
```
    8 8
X   9 9
_______
```

20.
```
    8 6
X   8 9
_______
```

Marks obtained: Comment:

1.
```
   6 2
× 3 1
______
```

2.
```
   6 9
× 9 6
______
```

3.
```
   1 3
× 6 0
______
```

4.
```
   6 3
× 1 2
______
```

5.
```
   6 5
× 4 9
______
```

6.
```
   7 8
× 5 5
______
```

7.
```
   5 2
× 8 9
______
```

8.
```
   5 9
× 2 4
______
```

9.
```
   7 8
× 2 3
______
```

10.
```
   9 8
× 4 2
______
```

11.
```
   6 8
× 7 3
______
```

12.
```
   5 5
× 8 6
______
```

13.
```
   9 6
× 4 5
______
```

14.
```
   3 2
× 8 3
______
```

15.
```
   6 9
× 8 2
______
```

16.
```
   4 8
× 1 9
______
```

17.
```
   2 9
× 9 9
______
```

18.
```
   8 1
× 5 5
______
```

19.
```
   7 1
× 8 4
______
```

20.
```
   3 5
× 7 7
______
```

102

Marks obtained: _______   Comment: _______

1.
```
    9 8
X   2 6
_______
```

2.
```
    2 4
X   6 6
_______
```

3.
```
    3 7
X   2 3
_______
```

4.
```
    7 4
X   5 0
_______
```

5.
```
    4 7
X   4 8
_______
```

6.
```
    7 1
X   1 8
_______
```

7.
```
    6 5
X   3 8
_______
```

8.
```
    7 7
X   9 8
_______
```

9.
```
    7 2
X   4 8
_______
```

10.
```
    3 5
X   8 4
_______
```

11.
```
    1 4
X   9 2
_______
```

12.
```
    5 3
X   6 2
_______
```

13.
```
    7 9
X   3 7
_______
```

14.
```
    4 7
X   6 3
_______
```

15.
```
    2 3
X   8 6
_______
```

16.
```
    9 6
X   3 9
_______
```

17.
```
    8 2
X   6 9
_______
```

18.
```
    4 9
X   4 9
_______
```

19.
```
    6 9
X   8 2
_______
```

20.
```
    2 9
X   7 8
_______
```

Marks obtained:　　　　　　Comment:

<table>
<tr><td>Name:</td><td></td><td>Date: / /</td></tr>
<tr><td>Marks:</td><td>TIMED TEST</td><td>Time:</td></tr>
</table>

1.

$$\begin{array}{r} 7\ 2 \\ \times\ 7\ 6 \\ \hline \end{array}$$

2.

$$\begin{array}{r} 6\ 6 \\ \times\ 5\ 8 \\ \hline \end{array}$$

3.

$$\begin{array}{r} 9\ 5 \\ \times\ 5\ 0 \\ \hline \end{array}$$

4.

$$\begin{array}{r} 8\ 2 \\ \times\ 4\ 7 \\ \hline \end{array}$$

5.

$$\begin{array}{r} 2\ 8 \\ \times\ 3\ 8 \\ \hline \end{array}$$

6.

$$\begin{array}{r} 7\ 4 \\ \times\ 8\ 8 \\ \hline \end{array}$$

7.

$$\begin{array}{r} 6\ 5 \\ \times\ 1\ 8 \\ \hline \end{array}$$

8.

$$\begin{array}{r} 4\ 3 \\ \times\ 8\ 1 \\ \hline \end{array}$$

9.

$$\begin{array}{r} 8\ 6 \\ \times\ 8\ 6 \\ \hline \end{array}$$

10.

$$\begin{array}{r} 6\ 8 \\ \times\ 5\ 9 \\ \hline \end{array}$$

11.

$$\begin{array}{r} 8\ 4 \\ \times\ 4\ 9 \\ \hline \end{array}$$

12.

$$\begin{array}{r} 5\ 2 \\ \times\ 9\ 2 \\ \hline \end{array}$$

13.

$$\begin{array}{r} 5\ 9 \\ \times\ 3\ 7 \\ \hline \end{array}$$

14.

$$\begin{array}{r} 1\ 9 \\ \times\ 8\ 5 \\ \hline \end{array}$$

15.

$$\begin{array}{r} 6\ 6 \\ \times\ 4\ 3 \\ \hline \end{array}$$

16.

$$\begin{array}{r} 7\ 7 \\ \times\ 1\ 9 \\ \hline \end{array}$$

17.

$$\begin{array}{r} 8\ 5 \\ \times\ 2\ 7 \\ \hline \end{array}$$

18.

$$\begin{array}{r} 5\ 5 \\ \times\ 4\ 9 \\ \hline \end{array}$$

19.

$$\begin{array}{r} 1\ 8 \\ \times\ 5\ 6 \\ \hline \end{array}$$

20.

$$\begin{array}{r} 7\ 6 \\ \times\ 5\ 3 \\ \hline \end{array}$$

104

Marks obtained:

Comment:

<table>
<tr><td>Name:</td><td></td><td colspan="2">Date: / /</td></tr>
<tr><td>Marks:</td><td colspan="2"># TIMED TEST</td><td>Time:</td></tr>
</table>

1.	2.	3.	4.	5.
2 9 × 1 6	3 3 × 2 6	3 5 × 8 3	2 6 × 8 2	3 8 × 6 1

6.	7.	8.	9.	10.
7 1 × 4 8	9 1 × 9 5	4 7 × 7 9	4 5 × 3 7	5 2 × 7 8

11.	12.	13.	14.	15.
2 9 × 5 8	6 2 × 7 5	6 4 × 4 9	6 7 × 2 8	3 7 × 8 6

16.	17.	18.	19.	20.
9 9 × 9 9	9 1 × 4 9	8 0 × 5 4	6 5 × 8 8	4 8 × 5 7

Marks obtained:

Comment:

OTHER BOOKS BY JOLPIC KIDZ